Brad Pitt's Dog

Brad Pitt's Dog

Essays on Fame/Death/Punk

Johan Kugelberg

zero
books

Winchester, UK
Washington, USA

First published by Zero Books, 2012
Zero Books is an imprint of John Hunt Publishing Ltd., Laurel House, Station Approach,
Alresford, Hants, SO24 9JH, UK
office1@o-books.net
www.o-books.com

For distributor details and how to order please visit the 'Ordering' section on our website.

Text copyright: Johan Kugelberg 2011

ISBN: 978-1-78099-502-1

A CIP catalogue record for this book is available from the British Library.

Cover Design: Will Swofford Cameron
Type Design: Lance Scott Walker

Printed and bound by CPI Group (UK) Ltd, Croydon, CR0 4YY
Printed in the USA by Offset Paperback Mfrs, Inc

We operate a distinctive and ethical publishing philosophy in all
areas of our business, from our global network of authors to
production and worldwide distribution.

Contents

For my family

The narratives in this book are small, they are of marginalia, of the minutia of everyday art and entertainment and how they wrap around each other like the branches of the blackberry plant, intertwined as our everyday very lives are, and also were, even back in the days when such devices (named by a clever cynic for the eversame reason) did not yet exist. Tiny, important, life-changing petty miracles and morsels occur over and over, statements of ecce humani generis (see all mankind) within our collective cultural landscape. All these moments, lost in time like tears in rain, Rutger Hauer said in Blade Runner. Here, some of the miniscule reverberations that have enshrouded themselves in my cervical vertebrae have been gathered and are told at random, which was how Simon Jeffes' described the on-goings at his Penguin Café, inspiring us to follow his illuminating example of how randomness, impermanence and a lack of grandeur are very important, and how these narratives considered as pop culture wabi-sabi help explain how big truths can reside within small things. A sense of the sublime located in the grooves of a copy of a 7-inch 45 of "To Find Out" by the Keggs or in a xeroxed and stapled Raoul Vaneigem pamphlet, or in your experience of a drawing by a child. Or surfing.

As we reach for the century of popular culture past that is stored close to our fingertips, we can sup on the nourishment that stems from these myriad human voices and the micro-history of their craft stored in song, in dance, in poetry, in art, in food and on and on and on. If we pay attention to what we can cull from up there on the screen, adding our notions of temporality and our visceral power of emotional will, then the limitations of the screen (or the printed page) can be transgressed and we can experience deep lore of deep yore with the same strength and somberness that we utilize when we remember the sound of the laughter of someone who is dead.

These essays were completed during the last ten years or so, after the twin towers fell, after my departure from the rapidly crumbling record biz (tout à fêtes!), and in parallel with my increased involvement in putting together books and staging exhibits. My main objective for the books and traveling exhibits that I continue to put together is the micro-historical reveal of the human dimension of the past.

The years 2005 through 2008 saw the realization of my work in the field of hip hop history: a traveling exhibit which lead to a book (Born in the Bronx, Rizzoli 2008) which in turn instigated our founding of the Cornell Hip Hop History Archive with attached symposium and curriculum. 2009 saw the publication of an artists' monograph I put together, devoted to a rock & roll band: The Velvet Underground: A New York Art and its accompanying traveling exhibit, culminating in a grand event celebrating the band, with Lou, Moe and Doug chatting informally in that snazzy golden room at the New York Public Library. By the time this book goes to print, my most recent work in micro-historical archiving will be announced from its permanent home upstate at Cornell University: the placement of a substantial archive devoted to the aesthetic history of the punk movement alongside an archive devoted to hip hop history feels pretty great, as both strands together came to pass as examples of the seismic shift of the late 20th century DIY spirit.

I hope that is where this book comes in, and that there is a theme to be found here on the importance of self-starter culture, the tiny revolutions of everyday life that are set in motion all around us at all times, how we need to cherish them, and how growth and realization stems from collective thinking set vigilantly against all the societal currents that attempt to shove us towards hyper-individualism.

The main inspiration for this book came from Timothy D'Arch-Smith's books: the sublime Peeping Through A Seafood Store and Books of the Beast, both yardsticks, and if you've read them, it'll be clear that student is student and master is master.

—Johan Kugelberg, NYC,
Summer 2011

I'd like to thank the following hepcats for their help with this book: Bob Stanley, Jack Womack, Jon Savage, William Gibson, Geoffrey Weiss, Michael Daley, Will Swofford Cameron, David Tibet, Jeff Gold, Gabriel Mckee, Katherine Reagan, Anne Kenney, Kevin Repp, Penny Rimbaud, Gee Vaucher, Peter Beste, Lance Scott Walker and Zero Books.

1

Michael Jackson is Dead, Alas…

Not the most original thought thunk, but in Procopius' *Secret History* and Petronius' *Satyricon* and in one of the Loeb's Cicero volumes there are plenty of examples why fat Elvis was ultimately more beloved than skinny Elvis: this Roman/American dream has a chunk of what Nietzsche's last man dreamed about: to wake up and know that all notions of good and evil live and die within the self. Jackson unleashed was Elvis unleashed, or Charlie Sheen or Errol Flynn or the empress Theodora, wife of Justinian. Indulging in erotically charged conduct with kids around wasn't wrong because he thought it right, the towering statue on the Thames and the entourage of enablers and the bananas real estate choices were more a general array of seduction tools than external impositions of internal grandeur. Justinian's human torches and Caligula's blood frescoes were congenial to the worth of the human life of a slave at that specific point in time.

Jackson fired lawyers/nannies/chefs and doctors.

Off with their heads!

People don't age in television re-runs or rock video downloads, so therefore there seems to be a business model to be set up where look-a-likes for the artists' prime-years can show up and conduct civil war re-enactments, and the artist/actress/model/porn-star can age in her mansion Sunset Boulevard-style, until their death-struggle can become an act of medial bravery. The star becomes disposable quickly, but the boomers who were the first to grow up with television and re-runs and pop-culture meta (also: the amount of early hip-hop lingo, gags, and cultural signifiers that arrived fully formed from network TV in that scene is baffling: Patty Duke, Addams Family, Jeffersons etc.), saw the Farrah Fawcett's and SNL-ers and rock video stars as their pop-cultural counter-point and dream-weapon, to be used against the history and tradition and responsibilities force/spoon-fed them by their parents and grandparents who never let them forget for a minute that they fought the war and sacrificed everything to provide them with color tv and 28 flavors.

The only handy counter-attack is to gain complete control of dreaming, as the greatest generation were powerless in dreams.

In dreams began irresponsibilities.

In the projects, there are myriads of people who live their entire lives as ghetto-superstars. The facade or armor can and will last a lifetime as long as the up-keep is meticulous. Michael Jackson is a failed ghetto superstar, since the upkeep of his facade was so sketchy that we actually found out about the pedophilia, the near-bankruptcies, the skin bleach and the records that didn't do so well.

A ghetto superstar would never blow it like that: he'd come out of his low-income pad dripping with facade and strut like a monument of unrealized potential, with a plethora of deals in play, constantly, without any of them ever needing to be realized, as unrealized potential is always de facto potent, and stuff that actually has happened can be judged by an audience to be flaccid or done or passé.

Brand new, box-fresh, shiny and expensive. The preppy look has always been current in the ghetto. The titles have always been borrowed from the annals of big business and gentry: The Duke of Earl, The Chairman, The Prez, The CEO.

There will never be a vintage clothing store in the inner city.

Ask a stylish big-city member of a minority group about second-hand clothes and they'll look at you with disgusted bafflement. If you look at the berserk shopping and interior design habits of Michael Jackson, they are consistently box-fresh. The antiques are mint-condition or replicas, the art commissioned follies worthy of Mad King Ludwig or Claudius, and the Michael Jackson home-interiors is where the superstar keeps up a perfect facade, for himself and his visitors.

All is folly, and Jackson's failing in the acquiring of a page-boy that wakes him in the morning by shouting "Sir! Do not forget that you are a man!" or victorious Saladin-style having an empty wood coffin carried in front him doesn't mean that he didn't sell shitloads of records and that people in the furthest far-aways from the streets of Manhattan/Los Angeles consider him a primary deity in their pop-culture cargo cult pageant. Now with death no longer the great equalizer, but instead where the hollow dried-up husk of existence gets replaced by the bright, shiny and eternally suave pop-meta icon of chink-free armor and flawless facade, the cargo cult is aptly arriving à la death of Lady Di(e) on the streets of Los Angeles, the perennial death-trip town where the tyranny of the new is the tyranny of the old and the sun shone lacking alternative upon the eversame.

2010

2

Daido Moriyama
A Photograph is the Result of a Momentary Thought

As celebrity culture, mass marketing and advertising are increasingly presented in imagery that is a mimicry of everyday life, the ultimately purely destructive force of this forgery can enslave our very eyeball. In Moriyama's work an antidote for this pop art society of façade can be found, ever as potent as the work of Raoul Vaneigem; an immersion into the stark melancholic beauty of the discarded moments of life at its most ordinary. When Moriyama crystallizes these moments, we understand that our commonality of experience, its under-pinning of beauty worship, and our collective attempts at the location of aesthetic worth are a component of our arsenal against a society of spectacle. Moriyama's pictures are our pictures. Their everyday selection, his logorrhea of the eye, slows down the pace of how we gaze at our own personal familiar environment. We can see our fate laid out in front of us, like the play-by-play of a chess game in a daily newspaper.

It is wabi-sabi as photography, where the traces we've made, the echoes of our time, infuse meaning into the discarded, the marginal, and the lost.

A distant dream, a scratched cooking pot, the sound of the laughter of someone who is dead.

Daido Moriyama was born in 1938, along with a twin brother who died when he was two. His father worked in life insurance. When Moriyama was only a couple of months old, the family moved to Hiroshima leaving the sickly infant behind with his paternal grandparents in the town of Ikeda, a coastal town that bore emotional residue for Moriyama his entire life. When Moriyama commenced working on arguably his most important project, *Memories of a Dog*, the narrative started in Ikeda. His childhood was spent in the town of Urawa, outside Tokyo. Moriyama mentions the chocolate and chewing gum that would get thrown to the children by GI's in passing jeeps as one of his strongest memories of the immediate postwar years. Otherwise there aren't clear memories in his palate from these, the darkest years of recent Japanese history; a time that is never to be repeated in the minds of the people who lived through it, a time that has very few available images.

In his mid-twenties, working as a photography assistant (just prior to becoming a freelance photographer), Moriyama encountered Kerouac's *On The Road*. In many interviews, he speaks about the value of chance encounters, of transition and of what the main character in Kerouac's novel refers to as having "seen" the road.

Moriyama describes his taking of photographs as being like how a Spitfire plane fires its machine guns. Rapid bursts of instinctive shooting, without view finder, without focus, and without knowing what the image is until the moment it is distilled in the dark room has commenced for him, and will last a lifetime.

He "sees" the road.

In 1968, photographer Takuma Nakahiri shows Daido Moriyama the first issue of his photography journal *Provoke*, and asks him to participate in the second issue. The iconoclasm and originality of this obscure publication has reverberated continuously for over 40 years.

"I was always irritated by photography being a tautology – how can you describe it? I used to be a photographer who interpreted things via language. And then Provoke *changed me." - DM*

The influence of William Klein's series of documentary photography books, as well as Warhol's 1968 Stockholm exhibit catalogue (basically a Klein imitation) were clear, but the work in *Provoke*, especially issue 2, like Captain Beefheart's *Trout Mask Replica*, Joyce's *Finnegan's Wake* or Duchamp's *The Bride Stripped Bare By Her Bachelors*, is art so insulated, so original, and so contextually devoid of its surroundings that it is hard to believe that it actually ever happened.

The narrative flow in the three issues of Provoke goes under the surface. Like texts by Joyce or Philip K. Dick, the narrative hits you in rapid bursts of energy: disjointed, blurry, strange with crazed leaps of faith and wild juxtapositions. Images, not words: I don't read Japanese, so I've only experienced the images in Provoke, not alongside the texts. The *Provoke* manifesto by Koji Taki, published in the premier issue, had to wait 31 years to see its first English translation. This is how it appeared in Andrew Roth and Glenn Horowitz's landmark *Provoke* catalogue:

"Photographs alone are not ideas. They cannot encompass the totality of a concept, nor have they the interchangeability of language. Yet, because of their irreversible physicality – moments of reality clipped by the camera – photographs inhabit a world that lies behind language, at times provoking the world of ideas. When this happens, language can overcome its own rigid conventions, transforming into new words, new meanings. Today, as words are severed from their material base, their reality, to flutter in space, we photographers must use our own eyes to grasp fragments of reality far beyond the reach of pre-existing language, presenting materials that actively oppose words and ideas. Thus we have to swallow a certain degree of embarrassment in order to give PROVOKE the subtitle: materials to provoke thought."

Provoke was a publication of photography that succeeded in stepping outside of time, which is what Ernst Jünger said was our collective reason for getting very drunk. When Daido Moriyama was asked about Takuma Nakahiri and *Provoke* he said: "We were drinking every day and putting down every photographer, denouncing everything around us." *Provoke* certainly captures this sentiment. It also captures something of the essence of extreme intoxication: The thin-skinned hyper-reality and blurred edges of the drunk, where all one's surroundings are simultaneously heart-achingly beautiful and grotesque.

"For me, photography is not a means by which to create a beautiful art, but a unique way of encountering genuine reality at the point where the enormous fragments of the world -- which I can never completely embrace by taking photos – coincide with my own inextricable predicament." – DM

Jack Kerouac wrote *On the Road*, on a continuous roll of paper, without the formality of having to insert a blank sheet of paper in the typewriter. Like we write now, on our laptops, where the page break is an anachronism and a ritual. I'd like to think that Moriyama never had to change rolls of film, that his capture of images was not diminished by a formality like running out and the forced time-out of replenishment. That what he chose to find was found, and what was lost was simply lost.

"What is the meaning of life in a world and among human beings as grotesque, scandalous, and accidental as the one in which I live and those with whom I interact?" – DM

I am considering the work of Daido Moriyama contextualized within the realm of the famous 'Naked City' map of Paris, executed by Asger Jorn and Guy Debord in 1957. The illustration of the psycho-geographical city landscape, where only the parts that resonate are included. The other ones are blanks.

Daido Moriyama's deeply felt humanism fills in such blanks.

A lovely feeling of everyday connection reverberates its emissions from the page. It is possible that the motif had no aesthetic value prior to it being framed by Moriyama, a value or non-value still not detached from the moment Moriyama took the photograph. History is what is happening, but an image of history is never what happened. This could be a matter of intent: It feels similar to what a drift through an unfamiliar city feels like. As we drift, we constantly frame the city with the wall of our eye, and the city frames us back with its wall of the sky. The city smiles at Moriyama, even when it is at its most wretched.

"We perceive countless images all day long and do not always focus on them. Sometimes they are blurry, or fleeting, or just glimpsed out of the corner of the eye. Our sense of sight, which is active all day long, cannot be constantly coming to rest." -DM

The corporate circus-trick of consumer as artist is partially responsible for the relationship today between the vanguard of photographers and the cool-branding industries of commodity. This is obsequious, fawning and sycophantic. The photographer ultimately holds the short end of the stick: the images can maintain a notion of complete artistic freedom, followed by a handsome check, but this nevertheless is still only hawking products like a salesman.

I wonder how it feels for a young photographer, chasing the corporate paycheck, to ponder the work of Ed Van Der Elsken, Daido Moriyama and Anders Petersen - all out-of-step with the mainstream, with lines clearly drawn between commercial and private work. Do they recognize them as saviors, the bearers of something precious? As masters? Is it so obvious that we bring with us a romantic Rousseau-esque dream of the picturesque as we gaze, bewildered and bedazzled at the vanguard imagery of the *Provoke* gang? We crave a nourishment we perceive as honest and true, if what surrounds us seems devoid of substance.

In 1972, Daido Moriyama issued the milestone book *Bye, Bye Photography, Dear (Sashin Yo Sayonara)*. This book took the shoot-from-the-hip fragmentation of *Provoke* even further: fragmented, blurry, oddly cropped and distorted images flow from the pages like a drunken and distant dream, mimicking the urban landscape à la Constant, drifting through consciousness with the blurry fascination of a farmer in the city.

Through the chain and cycle of one person's memories stimulating an entirely other person's memories, the memories of many people converge gradually into a world memory. – DM

Photographs are perpetual copies, said Daido Moriyama. The only good copies are the ones which show up the absurdity of bad originals, said François Duc de la Rochefoucauld (a few centuries earlier).

23

The activity of creating situations instead of exploring them was what Situationists claimed as their prerogative. Substituting passive existence (bad originals) with a creation of the fleeting moment of existence (good copies). The photographer chooses the situation, the viewer interprets this situation, and our hope is the synthesis and creation of a new situation of collective memory. The Dadaists claimed in 1916 that uncomfortable art mirrors the suppression of ecstatic enjoyment by the powers that be. The placement of imagery in a collective memory is the third means of counter-action, alongside the drift and the *détourné*.

Our current overt usage of pastiche dates back to pop art: more derivative, more accurate, more borrowed, ripped-off, all references to an idealized past: scanned, collaged, silk-screened, down-loaded, up-loaded, improved upon and edited. These are bad copies and the exact opposite of the work of William Klein, Daido Moriyama and Andy Warhol; three examples of original photographic thinkers creating good copies, copies that counteract the bad copies surrounding us, especially when said copies are informed by Klein or Warhol or Moriyama. *Memories of a Dog*, Moriyama's best known work in the USA, was published as a continuous narrative in the Japanese publication *Asahi Camera* starting in 1983. It was collected into a book published in Japan the following year, a US publication with Moriyama's poignant and Proustian autobiographical texts translated into English appearing in 2004. Moriyama's best known image, and a photograph that has reverberated through the world very much in line with the *Provoke* manifesto, is the photo of a stray dog, glancing at the camera with the *je ne sais quoi* of Satan just having blown his nose in the wall-to-wall carpeting. This image as a stand-out amongst Moriyama's massive body of work tells us a bit of how we feel as viewers, as participants in a collective memory, be it ours, Moriyama's, or the one that belongs to the mutt.

Some days our howl is that life is wretched, some days that life is wonderful. Inside the memories of a dog, that distinction never comes to pass, as everyday life is beautiful *and* wretched.

"The crushing force of time is before my eyes, and I myself try to keep pressing the shutter release of the camera. In this inevitable race between the two of us, I feel I am going to be burnt up." – DM

2008

3

Carl Johan De Geer
The Camera as Consolation

2009 brought the first international publication and exhibits devoted to the documentary photography of Swedish multi-artist Carl Johan De Geer. This is insane: it is as if the work of Ed Van Der Elsken or Masahisa Fukase would have remained dormant in its home country for over 30 years before anyone outsiders took note. And that is pretty much the story with Carl Johan De Geer's photography: one hyper-rare photo book, *Med Kameran Som Tröst*, was issued in 1980, spanning his work from the fifties up to the late seventies. Carl Johan De Geer, as a masterful Leica M4 snapshot giant à la Van Der Elsken or Moriyama, has the sacred ability to capture the anyday grit of everyday life and make it beautiful. The rumpled post-sex sheets, the crumbling façade of a building in its final fleeting moments before demo, the interiors of these buildings, where Stockholm-boho's in the 1960's and 1970's were making love and raising families, gives us a glimpse of a Sweden inhabited by people who are *the other*, whose life experience is impregnated with *otherness*.

Carl Johan De Geer was born in 1938 to absurd privilege and abject unhappiness as a member of one of Sweden's most powerful aristocrat families, and his parents showed no discernable interest in him or his siblings. He grew up on a grand country estate with his grandparents, went to art school in the late 1950's, and in an epic choice of rejection lives his life to this day as a perennial Swedish underground artist, working in counterpoint to the privilege of his surname, and simultaneously being notoriously noted by the societal and cultural elites (who sometimes overlap) in this duck-pond of a nation via that same last name.

The photography is superb, instinctive, and created completely without labor or pretense. Carl Johan De Geer's Leica M4 OCD led to the camera being present everyday and always, and for the people in his surroundings becoming completely used to its presence and him snapping away.

As Carl Johan likes to point out, he rarely photographed people he didn't know. Hence the intimacy and extraordinary melancholic vibrancy of these snaps of times and ways deceased. With 20/20 retroactive irony applied, the people that travel through these snapshots were in some instances to become the current movers and shakers of Swedish society, culture and politics: Marie-Louise De Geer (current head of the Swedish National Dramatic Theatre), Lars Hillersberg (satirical cartoonist), artists Lena Svedberg and Oyvind Fahlström, Bo-Anders Persson of psych legends Träd Gräs and Stenar, cartoonist Jan Lööf and mainstream newspaper critic Leif Nylen, to name but a few, were collaborators and compadres, working with Swedish underground publications such as *Puss*, *Huvudbladet or Gorilla*, organizing demonstrations, executing street art, bastions of Swedish originality that continue to reverberate to this day.

It is easy, living in Megapolis in the year of our Lord 2009, to stare oneself blind at the stylish swagger of 1960's counter-culture, and contrast what was directly lived with our world of representations. This can feed inactivity, as everything seems to already have been sung, spoken, tap-danced, ukulele'd or performance-arted, leaving the populace who missed out on those groovy times with a vague sense of living in an age occurring after the end of the world.

This is A. bullshit, and B. millenarianism. The people with first-hand knowledge of the groovy grooviness of the sixties are dropping like flies, a bunch of them already pushing up Amazing Technicolor Dreamcoat daisies. But as we still haven't been able to completely depart the 20th century, and as the whatzit around us is informed by Pop-Art and Punk-Art, and as the rapidly departing baby-boomers continue the life-lie that only certain years of this mortal coil truly mattered, we must study these remains of the sixties with great care. We need to be able to tell the wheat from the chaff. If we don't, we won't be able to distinguish these pathfinders in nations of followers, here or there, then or now. If we can't recognize the original voices, we won't be going anywhere at any point soon.

This is how an artistic voice as singularly brilliant as Carl Johan De Geer was quite obscure throughout the 1960's and 1970's, and up til now mostly unknown outside Sweden. For artists that don't have the ability to conduct the ritualistic mid-managerial games to venture outside the incubator-esque finality of Sweden's borders, their work may languish in obscurity as far as the outside world is concerned. Added is the curatorial frustration of recognizing superior obscure artists, and inferior well-known artists, but what are you gonna do? Happens all the time around my house. At least we are here now. Carl Johan is a healthy, creative and all-around delightful gentleman in his early seventies. His work in a variety of disciplines positively shimmers with inner light, whether said work was executed 50 years ago or last week. Today, we are enjoying his photography, next time we'll enjoy his fabrics, his paintings, his sculptures and his graphic design.

2009

4

Paul Williams's Crawdaddy: The Tabula Rasa of Rock Fandom

The tabula rasa of rock fandom is Paul Williams's *Crawdaddy* and Greg Shaw's *Mojo Navigator*. *Crawdaddy* was first, but to me that is not so important, as those games of who-came-first feel a bit premature (OI!). The roots of rock fandom in science-fiction fandom needs to be stated once in a while, and in the instance of the *Mojo Navigator/ Crawdaddy* divide, the first is fannish, the second is sercon—terms coined in science-fiction fandom. *Fannish* means by and about fans and fandom, *Sercon* means Serious and Constructive. *Crawdaddy* was very serious, from the very start. The brilliant mind of Paul Williams, filtering and philosophizing the brand new rock aesthetic, with an initial stanza coming from the Cambridge folk scene.

Crawdaddy hit the ground running in Spring 1966 Boston, a locale and time where the flower people had not yet turned the ideas and enthusiasms of the beatnik/civil rights/ bohemian tough-guys and gals (who sadly and ironically were the inspiration) into bought n' sold hippie commodities. The catalysts and originators that set the hippies in motion, in much the same way as Little Richard got things rolling for Pat Boone, were people with cultural roots that ran deeper. *Crawdaddy* and *The Mojo Navigator* truly are documents that link the beatnik us-versus-them with the passionate sense of infinite possibility that mid-sixties rock and roll provided for the people who experienced it first hand.

Reading *Crawdaddy* brings about a superb fly-on-the-wall feeling, and with 20/20 hindsight, we don't have to swallow the camels presented to us. The careerist hippies were already such when they were the Great Society and the Warlocks: just read the contemporary critics. The Diggers were amazing, the Velvet Underground were underrated, the Doors were amazing live, and the guys in the Mystery Trend felt disconnected from the Frisco rock scene. Read it as it happens, as it happened. You can still order a set of facsimile issues of *Crawdaddy* online, and there are plenty of *Mojo Navigator* articles reprinted in the Greg Shaw/*Bomp* book. It is easy, it is cheap, go and do it.

So: If we reach for primary sources—instead of the first faded then photo-shopped memorial simulacra of sixties and seventies survivors—then perchance we can take these second hand, third hand and fourth hand notions, spit out the camels and possibly only swallow a handful of flies: 1960's rock fandom doubtlessly begat seventies punk, begat rock journalism good and bad, begat freeform radio, and (more problematically) begat music blogging.

Something that I failed to discuss in my tome on retro-consumption culture, *Vintage Rock T-Shirts*, was how the absolute stagnant and blank event horizon of decade after decade of popular music appearing in columns with numbers in front of them, devoid of context, brings about an outlandish importance in presentation, and the money saved can be spent on hair, jeans, shoes and vintage rock t-shirts. This makes me think of a photo in an old pre-punk fanzine of Eddie Flowers wearing what looks like a homemade Dictators t-shirt. The spiritual implications of a teenager somewhere in the Midwest, circa 1975, wearing a band shirt for a group none of his friends, peers, or the girls he liked had ever even heard of are baffling. It is very difficult to think this through unless we acknowledge the science-fiction fandom roots of rock fanzines.

One of the key phrases in science-fiction fandom is egoboo, stands for ego boost: the warm fuzzy feeling you get when your fanzine gets a good review, when your fanac (fan-activity) letter to the BNF (Big Name Fan) editor of a pro-zine (professional fanzine) gets printed, and they don't think you are a fugghead (you figure that one out). Rock fandom *was* science-fiction fandom prior to punk. The rock fandom BNFs had been SF fans: Lenny Kaye, Greg Shaw, even Lester Bangs had dabbled in the world of science-fiction fanzines and SF conventions. The early days of rock fandom followed the manners of SF fandom almost to a tee: conventions, APA's (amateur press associations), the trading of 'zines, LOCs (letters of comment), feuds, sercon (serious and constructive) versus fannish (about fandom itself), FIAWOL (Fandom Is A Way Of Life) or FIJAGH (Fandom Is Just A Goddamn Hobby), it was all there, as were—à la comic book guy on the Simpsons—t-shirts that could only be understood by the already initiated. Eddie Flowers's *The Dictators Go Girl Crazy* t-shirt was his armor and his code. Like the beanie worn by the science-fiction trufan or the flying cut sleeves of South Bronx gang members.

The nature of social reality and the means to its transformation are not to be found in the study of power, but in a long clear look at the seemingly trivial gestures and accents of ordinary experience. And this is why the origin of rock fandom is important and why I cherish re-reading old issues of *Crawdaddy* or *Mojo Navigator* or the *Teenage Wasteland Gazette*.

Living in the Megapolis of unfiltered info that is our collective homes with its perma-blinking ever-wake screen to everything that is our laptops, it is almost impossible to understand how important publications like *Crawdaddy* were way back in the when. They were the distributors of information, of enthusiasm, the keepers of the flame and the counter-culture life-line for the provincial hepcats. They built bridges between regional scenes, they brought about record company attention for bands that otherwise wouldn't have gotten beyond their immediate region.

Paul Williams pioneered this. Chalk it up alongside all his other accomplishments.

2007

5

The Psycho-Geography of Record Fairs: Utrecht, New York's Wfmu, and London Olympia

The commodification of all forms of culture – turning all its aspects into saleable things – and the rise of mass communications led to revolutionary potential easily being diverted, sometimes turned reactionary. – Guy Debord

I.

Do we collect records awake or dreaming?

Are we fueled by what the ancient Greeks called *enthousiasmos*: the ecstasy of the soul when it is communicating with a deity?

What does a record fair mean?

What happens at the record fair?

How do we feel while we are there?

How do we feel when we anticipate it?

Where does its powerful allure come from?

How have things changed as we nowadays fester in alienated consumption on Ebay?

II.

Does it matter what time you get in to the record fair? Whether you get in at four o' clock for an extra 20 bucks, or if you arrive with the average joe at six o' clock?

Or for that matter, if you chum up to a dealer and procure a coveted pass in the guise of being his *helper*. You know: like Santa's little.

What records are found during that first two hours? What records are found during load-in? Rifling through a half-open box as the dealer subdues his cardiac-arrest in mid-shlep -- powerlessly reflecting that the only exercise he's had since hauling boxes at the last record fair is hauling boxes at this record fair.

What records are found during load-out?

Who are those members of the true lumpen proletariat of record fairs who pursue the bins at a leisurely stroll in the last hours of the last day of the fair?

Not only are they in true abject contradiction of the bump and grind of opening night, but blissfully indifferent to the feverish transactions fueled by existential urgency that in some cases took place before the dealer had even removed his records from the u-haul!

There is a certain never-say-die panache of subtle one-upmanship when you spot someone you remember as a hardcore collector from way-back strolling into the Wfmu fair at noon on Sunday (last day) carelessly flicking through a bin or two. Dark are the stories told around camp fires cross country of said careless stroller purchasing a copy of the Mystic Zephyr 4 album in the Wfmu station-benefit dollar bin on Sunday afternoon.

"True story," sighs the hobo-esque record dealer who told the tale, emitting air in small puffs from a pursed mouth.

Does desire get satisfied?

Is the strife of this love inside a dream?

Does the record sell for more on Ebay?
(the dealer dreads and the punter hopes)

Does the record sell for less on Ebay?
(the punter dreads and the dealer hopes).

Has a bumpkin rented a table on behalf of his family, selling the personal collection of his recently deceased uncle, the editor in chief of a prominent hippie-era underground magazine, pricing all records and artifacts at two euros each, with the exception of the records that are unplayed, and come with the press kit, in which case they are four euros, or in case they are on a small label he has never heard of in which case he is selling them for one euro each? Yes. Dare I say yes? And then I asked him with my eyes to ask again yes and then he asked me would I yes to say yes, and his heart was going like mad and yes I said yes I will Yes.

And then we awoke. Alas it was only a dream. All the world is a record fair, and we are rarely players, mere punters and portrayers.

I was sitting in a chapel, at the funeral of an acquaintance, noticing a long line of strangers cueing up to the coffin. The man at the front of the cue laid his hand on the coffin and exclaimed: "Excellent! Would do business again! Five stars!" He stepped away. The next man walked up: "Smooth transaction, great seller, thanks!" And the next one: "A great ebayer with great shipping and perfect communication! A plus!" This continued for quite some time. And then I awoke.

III.

The record fair with the most fear in the room is doubtlessly New York City's Wfmu. There are plenty of unspeakably great and wildly rare records in the room, all haunted by the translucent spectre of pure paranoid angst.

I whisper his name:

Popsike

I whisper his other name:

Ebay

And the other names:

The Most Unclean
The Little Whore
Beelzebub
Son of Perdition
Lucifer.

This specter sides up to the dealer, who is holding a vanity pressing he just took out of his box of records that he has yet to price.

He couldn't find any information on the record on-line, and not only does the record have a massive break on it, but also one song with a wild fuzz guitar solo, and one long tranced-out track with bongos and a flute.

A backpack wearing crate-digger wrapped in Evisu and Visvim with his record bag on wheels in tow asks him how much he wants for it.

He wipes the sweat from his brow.

How much do you want to pay for it?

I don't know.

How much you want for it?

Well it is pretty rare…

The specter is whispering in both ears simultaneously.

... I hear Cut Chemist is looking for it... I need to look it up on Popsike to see how much it is worth... It is on a Japanese comp... Maybe I should put it on Ebay... I wonder if someone has used the break... I shouldn't spend a lot on a record, the fair has just opened...

The complex inter-personal dynamic between these two gents could give Tove Jansson or William Faulkner a one for the money and a two for the record show. Whether you believe that the Ebay-demon is real, or assess him as a figment of our imagination, or for that matter, address the concept of the demon as a half-baked metaphor used by a slovenly writer for his pursuit of moral judgments, you gotta admit that M.R. James would have had something to say about the eerie and uncanny emotional landscape of the Wfmu record fair. Guy Debord would have flailed and shouted about its abject psycho-geography, spilling his calvados. And Pieter Bruegel would have pulled his pencil out and started sketching, and Jacques Brel would have written a lyric about lost souls mired in life-long paralysis.

But I jest, just a little bit.

A VG minus of jest.

IV.

This year, the Wfmu record fair was less rugged than it had been for many years. I am trying to understand why. The reheated pizza was still miserable. You couldn't buy coffee. The live radio broadcast transmitting from the event kept the already nasty booming slap of the noisy room marinating in a constant schmutz of avant-improv and free noise.

This was inter-spliced with the grating voices of the DJ's: 30- and 40-somethings who feel like they are 20-somethings. "Not that there is anything wrong with that," said the glass-house to the brick.

The dealers were in a particularly foul mood for the commencement of the fair, caused by the record load-in, which was seemingly based on cattle-loading techniques originating in Chicago slaughterhouses. The additional cause of the dealers' collective irritation being the habit of European crate-diggers to unpack their boxes for them, and not stopping when yelled at, as the diggers were all listening to particularly slamming break-beats on their Ipod headphones. There were also a fair share of dealers who were truly miffed that nothing was really selling, and that the quality and knowledge of the clientele had really gone down the toilet. This assessment of the record fair situation becomes formally executed earlier for each year that passes. Apparently the record held is a northern soul dealer who started bitching about this at the fair before the dealers were actually let in to set up. Notwithstanding all this and that and more, as I said, this year the Wfmu record fair was less nasty and I just realized why: The ultra-harsh fluorescent tube lighting of yore had been replaced by something slightly less harsh. Apparently the numerous fashion fairs that are held in the space had all complained that the light made the customers look grotesque. Oddly enough, with the splendid new lighting and all, some people at the Wfmu fair still looked a bit on the grotesque side, a tad, a smidge. Like they'd stepped out of a drawing by Pieter Bruegel. But I jest, I do jest.

V.

Utrecht, Utrecht, how do I love thee?

When I attempt to convince other New York dealers and collectors to just go buy a plane ticket already, and visit what I think is the best record fair in the world, my rap usually starts with the anecdote about the 6' 8" collector of Kim Wilde picture sleeves that sided up next to me as I was pouring over some bin at the Utrecht fair:

"Hallo! I am Dieter from Germany," he howled.

"Howyadoin," I mumbled.

"I am doing so good!" he bellowed.

"I have found so many today! So many Kim Wilde picture sleeve 45s! I collect Kim Wilde picture sleeves! What do you collect?"

For a split second the nasty Anthony Bourdain-style cynicism almost overtook me. You know the kind: where you choose to ridicule the enthusiasm of somebody else because what they like doesn't fit your perception of what is cool. A powerful and dangerous mindset which rules many roosts of white middle class boys, an often applied survival kit for the person who was bullied in school, themselves becoming taste-bullies, or in worst case scenarios, taste-nazis. Like Sonic Youth. Or *Vice Magazine*. I didn't fall in that trap.

"Kim Wilde! Cool!" I exclaimed. "I am looking for European disco 45s with ridiculous sleeve art," I told him.

"OK!" yelled Dieter, rainman-style. "I will tell you if I find some! Please tell me if you see really cool 45s by Kim Wilde!"

"Sure will," I replied.

Dieter wandered off, or rather, sauntered off. I watched his permed red hair bop down the record fair alleyway, disappearing behind a couple of Matrix-goths. I remember thinking how unbelievably psyched I was that I had met Dieter, and how Dieter's raging enthusiasm for an artist best described as marginal was exactly the kind of holy quest that acted as a solid counter-weight to the kind of besserwisser mentality that usually reigns at record fairs. But then I started looking around: there were Dieters everywhere. Even the sour British psychedelic fatso dealers had a certain *je nais c'est quoi* of merriment that the very same dealers

41

certainly were devoid of at the London record fair a couple of weeks later. Why was this? Well: it is Holland. The Dutch have an extremely old merchant class, and with that, they have the aspirational refinement and tolerance of said class. You don't want to piss off customers, notwithstanding who those customers are, what they believe or what color their skin has. You also want to make sure that the success of your business leads to your kids having a better life than you, which means that knowledge, or how knowledge is stored, is respected whether it is books or records or paintings or ledgers or museums. It can also bring about a cosmopolitan hedonism, which is also good, international ideas of what is arousing, amusing or intoxicating brought to you by people from all over the world, trading in your most splendidly international ports.

VI.

The fair is tightly run, very professional. It is held in the middle of a ridiculously huge mega-complex that this very same weekend holds a giant sale of collectibles (Dutch kitsch rivals that of Ohio) as well as a book fair and a comic book fair, which means that if your attention deficit disorder is keeping you in check that day, you can wander away from the vinyl and Dieter, to enjoy the company of Dieter's friend who is the world's foremost collector and dealer of Rice Krispie box prizes (did you know that Snap, Crackle and Pop are Knisper, Knasper and Knusper in Dutch?). Look! His neighbor who will provide your life-span need for Italian erotic comic book figurines.

I am hard fetched to come up with a true downside to the Utrecht Record Fair. The closest I get to bitching is about the food, but the Dutch fast food also fascinates. It truly is in the spirit of Pieter Bruegel and Hieronymus Bosch: it is grotesque. There are three foodstuffs avoided by the international record dealers, and eagerly gulped by the Dutch: Frikandellen, Kroketten and Waffles. The Waffles are gigantic and drenched in syrup, powdered sugar, sugary preserves, chocolate and whipped cream. They are what you think people eat at the county fair. I'd argue that the smacked-out sugar OD would even intimidate an eleven year-old boy. Frikandellen are extremely fucked up: a rectangular chunk of minced mystery meat (pork? chicken? cow? alpaca?) deep-fried not so much to golden perfection, more to gray/brown grease-bombage. The dense rectangle is then sliced down its length, smothered in peanut sauce, and served on a bun. Fucked. There are rumors that the peculiarly Dutch curry-flavored ketchup is also utilized. The Kroketten is (or can be) minced chicken or pork mixed with mashed potatoes, béarnaise sauce and vegetables, coated with a splendidly thick batter and then having its daylights fried out of it. The taste is oddly breakfast cereal-esque, with an added specialty flavoring of White Castle onion rings. Pretty damn scary. The international dealers sustain themselves on French fries. But beware: If the Dutch are left to their own devices, and the lionshare of the fast food professionals at the record fair are Dutch, they'll smother your fries in what they call "frit saus." This is mayonnaise as we know it. Adding a layer of fat to the layer of fat. The never-say-die battle cry of junk food connoisseurship as your arteries are visibly hardening for each and every terminal bite.

VII.

There are records everywhere. Records records records. In the morning of the Friday, which is dealer day and setup day at Utrecht, the vitality of the airspace is positively shimmering. People from all over the world are unpacking their wares. Overseas dealers are pacing the floor waiting for their international expedited parcel full of rare vinyl from their home country. Records that aren't that rare in their home country, but that hopefully will fetch a fortune here in Utrecht. Plane tickets, hotels and meals are dear, so one must hope that the Peruvian, Brazilian and Mexican dealers have a mark-up of at least a few thousand percent. I hightail it over to the Mexican dealers first. Almost every year, I've found something special: talismans of pure magic, that sort of thing, usually in scratchy VG- condition, with picture sleeves as

43

distressed and faded as the bizarro-world denim of upscale boutiques. There are rare records and then there are rare records, and then there are fucking rare records: As my collection of Mexican 70's punk is completed by the acquisition of the *Rock en el Chopo* triple-LP, I marvel at the absurd ecstasy of this endorphin-rush, set in motion whence internet rumors, old discographies and fanzine articles gel together on the ol' want-list, reaching acme as a scratchy and worn Moby Dick is harpooned by an Ahab with coffee-jitters, 8 am on a Friday morning in a sleepy Dutch town.

VIII.

As salted and peppered veterans of the interweb all know, spend enough nighttime hours far from the bed of your loved one, bent over in front of the pale demon white glow of the screen, ebaying away in your undermost wear, and you'll find most of the records that were listed as "top wants" on that piece of paper tacked up on the bulletin board of the dorm room of your youth. All you need is cash, cash is all you need. Misfits singles, mint copies of albums by the Monks, the Sonics, the 13th Floor Elevators, the private press version of "Strings of Life," a Beatles butcher cover, Velvet Underground and Nico in mono with unpeeled banana, easy as long as your paypal account can withstand a couple of grand. The ebay listings that utilize phrases like "impossibly rare" are plentiful, but how can the record be "impossibly rare" when it is right there, in front of you on the screen, with a buy it now of 1200 bucks? Popsike then tells you that five copies have been sold in the past year, so what is impossible is possible, even when the dealer tells you that it is de facto impossible, at least five times in the past year.

IX.

I witnessed a bit of what seemed like a healthy record gloat at Utrecht. Small packs of collectors, who had arrived at the record fair together, on a sacred quest as such, would upon finishing their 8-hour exploration sit down together for a show and tell, interspliced with bites of tenderly deep-fried frikandellen and kroketten. Their shimmering greasy fast food providing a pleasant visual counter-point to their cyber-goth clothing, or their original Sisters of Mercy 45s. This seemed healthy. It gave the record fair a natural end- zone, a coda, a moment of reflection before the spoils of war were brought home to the turntable. Oddly enough, at Wfmu, I didn't see a lot of the sharing and gloating of spoils. Certainly, the lack of a café, and the general lack of space (this is NYC after all), didn't provide a physical locale for the end game, but I sensed that some of the collectors did hoard like lost children, lacking in this aspect of the situation. I imagine that a couple of pirates would have shown each other the sum of their pillage after they had sacked and burned some Caribbean shore town. Or maybe this too, is the demon/ spectre up to no good, whispering "Hush! Keep your records to yourself! They don't need to know! You got the record, your precious!" This truly mirrors the alienated consumption of Ebay. Your selection is anonymous, you bid under a pseudonym and you unpack your precious treasure alone. So thank god for record blogs, where you can hype your recent finds, and attempt to increase their worth through the osmosis of the sound-file. This sometimes back-fires as records described as KBD punk monsters on the blog or in the Ebay description have sounded a bit like poorly played REO Speedwagon to these ears, and described "Acid Folk masterpieces" have come across like James Taylor or the hippie couple in Mike Leigh's "Nuts In May." Pure gloating is also an option. An obsessive Swedish psychedelic fatso posts photos of his latest rare record finds, like others post photos of their cats or their grandchildren. This comes across as a bit sad, lonely and unhealthy. I'd rather hang with the goths and their frikandellen.

X.

At record fairs, with portable turntable in hand, and if God and the dealer allow it, you have the opportunity to sample the wares, like you can do at all excellent used record stores, and never at the bad ones, a useful yardstick. Same can be used at the fair: The dealers who won't let you drop the needle, for some reason, are usually the ones devoid of bargains. I couldn't find one dealer at London's Olympia record fair that readily and willingly let me sample their wares. This might possibly be as British dealers and collectors seem to be the vanguard pathfinders in the rarified field of the struggle against the second law of thermodynamics. In this world-view, the striving towards mint condition counter-acts our natural world of entropy, gravity and how mint becomes VG becomes G as in grave. A spurious moment along these lines was when a European record dealer listed a copy of the first Jefferson Airplane album in the Mint Plus condition in one of his record lists. Was it God's own copy? Had someone snatched it from the Platonic idea of the pressing plant? When it comes to original copies of popular 60's rock records, it seems as if the importance of the condition of the vinyl is contradicted by the physical well-being of the people who are safe-guarding their sixties memories through the collecting of artifacts. The records, posters and Beatles autographs are doubtlessly relics of the time of their lives, infused with such a potent voodoo of nostalgia that the psychotic amounts of emotional projection that is fixed on them is starting to be reflected by the stars themselves. One needs only to go to the grotesque Who documentary DVD *Amazing Journey* to hear a bunch of propped-up geriatric rockers inflict godlike self-importance upon the viewer, comparing their stage ass-wriggling and studio knob-twiddling with the people who actually did something actually important during the same era. That the sixties survivors believe steadfastly that what they did was for the better good of the world, instead the commodified expression of the spectacle that it was, is very sad. Autographs, posters, vinyl records in mint condition, saleable things infused with nostalgia, are not necessarily a bad thing. We drink a vodka drink and sing songs that remind us of our good times, but where the problem lies is where a period of time in your life is pin-pointed as the only one directly lived, and the remainder of your days being devoted to a representation of said times. The trickle-down of the 1967 yippie attempt to levitate the Pentagon in 2007 is the attempt of a sizeable crowd at a Rolling Stones or Led Zeppelin concert to elevate a truly leaden sixties rock reenactment.

The Spruce Goose won't take off, but we can pretend that it will. Even if the performance of the aging rock dinosaur is VG minus at best, his haberdashery isn't, his conduct isn't and his appearance on a mint copy of *Get Yer Ya-Yas Out* isn't. The mood at the Olympia Record fair was defeatist. It was as if the collective dealers and punters had woken up in May of 1945 and found out that they were lieutenants in the SS. There were murmurings that amazing finds of extremely rare records had occurred during the first half hour of the fair, but all this had happened to other people. Besserwisser psychedelic fatso and blog-toad records were legion, but they were all priced within an inch of the price-guide. I couldn't help but notice that the equivalent of the Utrecht punter show and tell herein dwelled within a dealer showing another dealer his fanciest stock before he took it home again. Like a livestock competition, except that the holder of the most beautiful steer or the largest pumpkin would take home a blue ribbon, where the record dealer had to make do with a bit of upmanship and gloat before the mint copy of *Odessey and Oracle* was put back into the box for another year.

XI.

History has ended, and what was once directly lived has now receded into a representation. Be it the nightly civil war reenactment of 30-year-old gigs at the Masque, the Mabuhay, CBGB, or the 100 Club that take place in most major cities as we speak, or the Myspace pages of 50-something punk legends who hung out at the Mask, Mabuhay, CBGB or the 100 Club back then and won't let us forget it. They'll never die, as they are punk rockers, and as punk will apparently never die, neither will they. What do we do then? We gossip about Black Randy on our blog. We glance at pictures of Penelope Houston from 30 years ago and sigh. Forty years ago it was called camp. People looked at photos of Mary Pickford and Douglas Fairbanks and sighed. Susan Sontag wrote a good book about it. This was while the Seeds, Velvet Underground and the 13th Floor Elevators were having brand new records out. The people who were sighing over Pickford and Fairbanks weren't swooning over the Velvets or the Seeds. Rather the opposite. And us, we never die, we collect those records, immersed in the sweetness of obsession aimed at a time and place that we certainly participated in with our breath, but certainly not with our bodies. It is not uncommon among fanatical record collectors to spend the span of their collecting career immersed in the years they just barely missed.

Some collect the romanticized trickle-down experiences of their older brothers and sisters, some collect the sounds surrounding the years of their actual birth, and some collect what they felt immersed in the zeitgeist of, but could not follow through as lifestyle, usually due to age, sometimes due to geography. This is bittersweet: It is possible that the collecting instinct stems from an attempt to reconnect to the very moment when art opened your mind to the endless possibilities of human expression for the first time. I think it started for me around the age of five, à la "Rock & Roll" by Lou Reed, and then kept gaining strength (momentum) up until the catharsis of puberty brought punk rock seven-inchers within the general ballpark of Dogtown skateboards, Levi's 501's and Vans sneakers in commodity fetishism. Three events particularly warped my fragile little mind: The son of my nanny, Swedish rocker Peter Torsen, leaving his copy of *the Velvet Underground and Nico* and his issues of *Zap Comix* within my reach when I was very small. Attending the Don and Moki Cherry children's jazz workshop at Stockholm's Museum of Modern Art circa '70/'71, and listening to a radio show called *Asfaltstelegrafen* commencing broadcast in Sweden circa 1976, where the sandwiching of pub rock, 60's punk, punk and 50's rock & roll was presented as if that was a natural thing, which at that point in time it certainly wasn't. This led me directly to the mind-blowing lifeline of rock & roll fandom, since I spent a chunk of my teenage years in a village of a few hundred people close to the arctic circle. Between rock fandom and skateboarding, an outsider status that unlike that of science-fiction fandom wasn't necessarily anathematic to success with girls, branded me (some would say scarred) for a life of record collecting. Skateboarding I gave up after a particularly nasty fall in 1999.

I still miss it though.

XII.

Our emotional projection on the artifacts that remain of our youth's cartoon rebellion is supposed to necessitate our belief system of extended adolescent self-worth. The hedge-fund lower- upper- management aging hardcore kid spending upper four figures on Misfits test-pressings is battling the same laws of gravity that middle-aged women struggle against at the plastic surgeon or the cosmetics counter. This battle, masking as against grave and aging process, and against gravity itself, constitutes one of the most necrotic abrasions into the body-fabric of our very existence: this perpetuated falsity that only certain years in our life-span really truly matter. That life in our youth is worth so much more as a commodity, that once youth passes us by, we are obliged to forfeit what we directly lived and recede into a representation of said years for the remainder of our actual duration. Our choice of appearance, our choice of the most meaningful artifacts we surround ourselves with, our choice of the record we place in double plastic bags in alphabetical order, all representing time we address as lived in qualitative actuality.

XIII.

What sounds stream through our ears in our homes is very important, but more important is our choices of what sounds are to be streaming. The significance of the sound-event supersedes the experience of the sound-event. Whatever you do, don't sell the records. It might be tempting to buy a Volvo station wagon or a bigger apartment that can hold both your dog, Iggy, and your first-born, Syd. Don't do it. Look at your stereo, stare into the vortex of your turntable and remember that silence equals death. Even if you don't listen to your vinyl anymore, the idea of being able to spill that copy of 'Love At Psychedelic Velocity' you once thieved onto the turntable means that the disc *isn't* gathering dust on your record shelf; it is *levitating*. Wicked gravity can't hold it down, as it can't hold you down, so the rare record or the botox injection as elixir of youth certainly does do the job you intend it to, but beware, the fix gets quicker and quicker, and you need more and more! We all enter the labyrinth and we build our own maze as we venture further into it, and such can the metaphor for life and/or record collecting reverberate. But does it have to be a labyrinth? Can't it just be a repast, a good thing, a source of strength, a means of meditation? Sir Toby's hobby-horse in *Tristram Shandy*, utilized by us all as a source of order when that is in short supply in our everyday life, or for that matter, as a source of disorder when we need some more of that to get through our book of days. I could think of worse use for empiricism than record collecting: Once the choices have been made of what sounds are to stream through our ears in our home, they can commence to stream, at least after the mailman has arrived and before we place them in double plastic bags.

XIV.

I wonder if Utrecht, Wfmu and London Olympia are entrances to the labyrinth, or if they are milestones within it, or mill-stones around our neck, or (gasp!) exits or perhaps toll booths? Are we lusting for death, death itself? Are we incapable of considering the passing of time? Or is it the opposite? Are record fairs well and truly Limbo, now that the catholics have given up their copyright claim, or should that be territorial claim? Have we brought Limbo into our homes? Does the instant graft-grift or grift-graft of an Ebay-win and the gratification we hope for not ever arrive at all? Camus' Sisyphus is only ever stoked about the rare KBD-punk 45 he just won as he is logging on to bid on other records, the physical arrival in the mailbox of the actual record only reminds him of rolling boulders (his day-job) in order to afford to win other auctions.

XV.

Sometimes the map is on the territory and sometimes the map *is* the territory. As a turntable thrill-seeker, I will doubtlessly be going to plenty of record fairs for the remainder of this mortal coil. With the self-inflicted music biz disaster of digital downloading, vinyl is going to be collected and the Rolling Stones are going to symbolize rebellion for another century at least. Is this an ecumenical matter?

Maybe.

As I haven't really answered any questions in this whiff of an article, I might try to do so now, at the very end. So here:

Q: Do we collect records awake or dreaming?
A: We collect them awake, but we hope that the records will make us dream.

Q: Are we fueled by what the ancient Greeks called *enthousiasmos*: the ecstasy of the soul when it is communicating with a deity?
A: No.

Q: What does a record fair mean?
A: It means that alienated consumption isn't that great.

Q: What happens at the record fair?
A: A lot of men venture further from their goal of having plentiful sex by looking for records that quite often sing about plentiful sex.

Q: How do we feel while we are there?
A: We salivate as our head gets struck by a mallet.

Q: How do we feel when we anticipate it?
A: We certainly salivate less.

Q: Where does its powerful allure come from?
A: The physical impossibility of death in the mind of someone living.

Q: How have things changed as we nowadays fester in alienated consumption on Ebay?
A: Finding a copy of the Spunky Spider 45 for less than 100 pounds means going through vast quantities of bargain bin 45s.

2007

6

The New Sincerity

It is not impossible that the new sincerity trend came out of a generation of youth living in dialectic betwixt media and oblivion where the epiphanous notion that being hip has no value fueled a gigantic appetite for meaning, meaning as midwifed by consumption.

I note that the decline of irony in the fade to grey years of neo-con came with a counter-thrust thirst for insignia and indicators of authenticity. As the applied irony and blog/web/gawker-comment box snide is being back-lashed with the (in some instances) equally hollow white middle-class pose of the new sincerity, it is of merit to attempt to identify the ideas of these new Ides of March: the much more subtle gloat of betterment is the rejection of cultural and spiritual superiority as a weapon lacking ammunition.

Every time I chuckle as some exponent of the new sincerity strides past me I immediately feel a bit bad and attempt to stifle it. There's no doubt that the new sincerity is a good thing as in Martha says: urban 20-somethings making homemade dill pickles, buying vintage vinyl, dressing in tweed and rocking Louise Brooks-smocks as they earnestly discuss Faulkner or Bataille is pure and unfiltered *A Good Thing*. I need to thwart any suspicion that they *en masse* were trucker-cap-wearing coke-snorting skinny-jeans Vice types mere months ago. That can't and shouldn't be the case. No sir.

Back in the while ago, as I was working on a book on hip hop, I had an epiphany which I think is of some worth: observing suburban homeboys in Greenwich, Connecticut, I noticed how my irritation was replaced by awe. Instead of fidgeting about the shmuckiness of affluent white boys and white girls dressing, speaking, and walking *ghetto* I came with bafflement to the conclusion that our Connecticut friends were emulating a culture they perceived as authentic, and that it provided an emotional anchoring and authentic life in an environment that they perceived as inauthentic.

They were rejecting their phony society and its false values and venturing into a lifestyle that made them feel a part of something *real* that brought them a sense of community. Cue the new sincerity.

As counter-cultural lifestyle elements became resume-builders and career-development fodder via the grunge/alternative boom of the early nineties, I think a parallel narrative germinated as a result, blooming in our day and age as The New Sincerity. The members of Vampire Weekend, Yea-Sayer and their sartorially splendid ilk were born right around the time of Pavement and Liz Phair, and will on some level have had their pre-teen years infused with alternative lethargy and the defeatist residue of a smashed pumpkin. The aesthetic choices made by the alternative generation, the prozac, the all-slave-ethic-all-the-time lyrics of the everyfolk grunge super stars and their twee-rock alt brethren infused the kids growing up in the late 90's and 00's with something to act in opposition to, especially as the alterna-grunge kids reinvented themselves as electro-clashing hedonists soaking in the splendor of a boom-economy where *everyone* wanted a website designed and *every* corporation thought that hiring an edgy stylist to supervise the photo shoot for their in-house dental plan information folder was a great idea.

Alterna-grunge + dotcom loot = electro-clash/sarcastic moustache.

Can we agree on that?

Furthermore,

Keeping-it-real-sideburns < sarcastic mustache < tender lover beard.

Can we agree on that as well?

Pat Boone + The Strokes = Vampire Weekend.

That too?

And when it comes to the Freak Folk/New Weird America craze, and its abject ultra-sincerity, can we deduce that civil war re-enactors in period hippie garb, recording on period reel-to-reels, growing period-scuff facial hair and (no doubt) stifling their period flow with period feminine hygiene products are utilizing exactly the kind of life-raft, in fact clawing at the raft, as these young peoples have had far too many day-hours of their formative years self-surgically attached to dully glowing blue screens? They are in their own way putting up a struggle against the screen-life through the utilization of these authentic tokens of real life of yore. Over-the-hillbillies like me claim that what was once directly lived has receded into an abject representation.

The importance of connoisseurship has never been more prevalent in an urban cultural strata than among the new sincerity crowd. You need to know a lot. A whole hell of a lot. Luckily, the level of knowledge you need to amass is along the lines of an Edwardian occult order: You can front as long as it seems as if you know. Your knowledge of the first five seconds of songs in any given underground music genre is legion. Your perusal of trailers of marginal genre films reached four digits, and your apparent expertise in the field of Japanese hand-made and hand-dyed denim is on par with a lifelong professional. At least as long as we live in a world of appearances, which we do. The naming of things is the knowledge of things, and it makes you wonder if the naming of the jeans-spirits, rock-spirits, tree-spirits and artisan cheddar-spirits, as the new sincerity crowds walk through life like hunters and gatherers, is the only self-empowerment left to those who have their everyday infused with a world of banal appearances on Facebook pages and message boards.

You can root around on FFFFound and stare yourself google-eyed on rollicking brigades of global eye-hyper-candy, all providing visual stimuli that winks come-hither hollow-promise-style as it hints of visceral experiences with the texture of cozy fabrics and the scents of aged cheese, of pornographic consumer choices that can evermore only titillate, until the very essence of your being demands to spurt out in a throbbing cataclysm of shopping for products that seem to fulfill all those innermost urges and cravings of sincerity, authenticity, textures, smells, history and a context of you and your kind as propagators of the WIN of life, not the EPIC FAIL of the decline of empire and the crumbling collapse of carefully crafted manufactured goods.

We must also remember that these are the habits of children: The men take enormous pride in their ability to grow facial hair. The foodstuffs that new sincerity restaurants and grocery stores obsess over are all landmarks of a childish palate, connoisseurship of bacon, meat, cheese, deluxe junk food, cereals, oats, preserves, pickles. The clothes are manly and womanly in manners that mimic kids playing grown-ups. I think this has to do with the lack of transitional time between being a debauching teenager and a debonair young adult. Once you are in college, you feel the urge to define yourself as worldly, knowledgeable, a connoisseur of the fine things in life, but as your palate (aesthetic as well as actual) is that of a child, your choices of indicators of refinement remain those of childhood. I can't but wonder if the new sincerity demand for immediate answers to questions of commodity consumption is based on an unsure reality that is now obliged to give us immediate answers since that is how our online life chugs along on Wikipedia and its brethren of immediately authoritative misinformation.

Problematic as all heck, yep, as our experience of the news reporting surrounding the Japanese tsunami and nuclear accident came to prove that hyper-fragmented news updates presented at a pace so frantic that the ordinary checks and balances of news reporting were now just as dislodged as the plug and socket of the nuclear power plant or the mish-mashy pseudo-scholarly megalomania of the Wikipedia editing process. I think this will ultimately truly extend the lifespan of the new sincerity trend. These 20- 30-somethings are programmed to extend their emotionally rewarding consumption to how all manners of information is consumed. It is already happening. Turn over a rock and another octavo-sized journal is published on uncoated stock, featuring artisanal fashion brands, musings on 19th century lit, unfocused snapshots of skinny people hanging out in authentic country surroundings, and lists of where you can go and buy gear that caters to this self-revealing lifestyle. I am sure that we are a leap and a skip away from news-reporting and event-reporting with a similar slant, away from the pulsebeat of the online din, published as letterpress broadsides, announced in the hamlets of upstate New York with loud yells of "Hear Ye! Hear Ye!" As ol' Guy Debord proved in *We Turn In The Night Consumed By Fire*, turning away from the world and its deceitful chatter is one of the high-points of bourgeois luxury consumption.

2011

7

No More Jubilees

Kilburn and the Highroads "Rough Kids" was the first punk single.

No, Patti Smith's "Piss Factory" was the first punk single.

No, "Politicians In My Eyes" by Death was first.

No, King Mob did it first.

No, Suburban Press did it first.

No, Guy Debord did it first.

No.

History is elastic. As soon as you attempt to pinpoint a date when things started, evidence to the contrary magically appears. Punk's origins are especially contentious.

In the early 70s, as the people who had the money and the corporate affiliations were the ones making music, rock & roll became an ordinary social fact, like a commute or a highway construction project. It became a habit, a structure: The Doobie Brothers, Three Dog Night, James Taylor, Toto, Linda Ronstadt. The chaos in society called for music of permanence and reassurance: renderings of small problems or the life of ease of rich solipsist rock stars. This fed itself with success like an Ouroboros who kept on eating not noticing the bland and somewhat putrid flavor. As meaningless as the choices of fast food at the mall food court. As wretched as the chicken in a bun under the heat lamp. The negation of boredom was the duty of sociopaths said the Situationists and gave birth to the punks.

History is written by the winners. Or the losers 30 years later. Or the ones who were neither winners nor losers and weren't really there at all but who became obsessed with the *zeitgeist* of what they just missed out on, which would be me. I was too young for punk, but certainly caught the bug in the most severe way imaginable thanks to the cruel fate of having only just missed it. A lot of ink is being spilled here, a new retrospective of seminal punk history rears its (balding) head every 30 minutes. These anniversaries range from the truly meaningful (30 years since the Pistols, the Clash, and the Buzzcocks played the Screen on the Green) to the splendidly meaningless (30 years since John the Postman bought a copy of the first Hammersmith Gorillas single), to the arbitrarily meaningless (what was the first punk record?). The meaning that we infuse these strands of pop culture spectacle with, or the simplifications that we cookie-cut to a historical mold, are the eversame falsifications of historical record the winners or losers or not-there-at-alls of pop culture history are slowly fattening our livers with, foie-gras-style.

History re-writ makes heroes of opportunists (the Clash spring to mind) and originators out of brilliant hustlers (we love Malcolm!). The 20/20-hindsight edit has the first Ramones album setting the template with no mention that its innovations where shoplifted from the Dictators *Go Girl Crazy*, released the previous year. *Sniffin' Glue* became "the first punk fanzine" six months after the debut issue of *Punk* magazine and six years after the late, great Alan Betrock wrote a Punk Rock Consumer Guide in his fanzine Jamz. Caroline Coon originated the phrase punk in the pages of *Melody Maker* circa mid-1976, but a concert flyer for New York's gods of art-skronk, Suicide, dated December of 1970 bears the legend "Punk Music by Suicide." As Johnny Rotten re-constructs his de-constructed jacket with safety-pins in 1976, a Warhol-scenester does the same in 1968, mimicked by Richard Hell in 1973, as do Cleveland art-skronk demons the Electric Eels, in 1974 (the latter gaining extra punk points for using rat-traps in place of safety pins).

When the glorious mod-meets pub-meets glam-meets-Johnny Burnette power-chord din of Steve Jones blazed forth from his white Les Paul at the Delmar Street rehearsal space in the spring of '76, it echoed the ragged shards of broken glass from Doctor Feelgood's Wilko Johnson.

Wilko mimicked Kilburn and the Highroads guitarist Keith Lucas, who after the '76 punk explosion became Nick Cash of the band 999, a superb example of music hall-esque punk a la Matlock-era Sex Pistols. The first megastar backlashes of British music in the 1970's were Dr. Feelgood and Kilburn and the Highroads. With said perfect vision of hindsight, one can view the packaging of Dr. Feelgood's debut *Down By The Jetty*, see the short hair, the stark chiaroscuro image, the wearing of grimy narrow suits and grimier, narrower ties. The sulphate-fueled aggro concealed within, pointing toward the sound of punk to come.

Tommy Roberts, creator of the slogan t-shirt that he marketed in the late 1960's at his shop Mr. Freedom, address 430 Kings Road, managed Kilburn and the Highroads, starting the job in July of 1974. He met Ian Dury through his acquaintance Malcolm McLaren. *The Rocky Horror Picture Show* was playing down the Kings Road and Kilburn and the Highroads played a weekend of gigs at that same theatre, amidst the bondage gear and rubber sex clothes. Kilburn and the Highroads were a chaotic rock'n'roll band with a singer that couldn't sing hunched over a microphone stand like Quasimodo, glaring angrily at the audience. This is how a blur of footnotes can erase the lines between eras and epochs, landmarks and watersheds.

"Everywhere, youth (as it calls itself) discovers a few blunted knives, a few defused bombs, under 30 years of dust and debris; shaking in its shoes, youth hurls them upon the consenting rabble, which salutes it with its oily laugh."
— Advertisement for *Potlatch* in *Les Levres Nues* 1954

There are no lines to be drawn. The punk rockers that used to speak and act with panache and swagger are now devoted to protecting and defending their identity as punk rockers. The problem with this is as we know that a fixed identity weakens the original stance and strengthens the spectacle. Asger Jorn said that every avant-garde grows old and dies without seeing its successors, because succession doesn't follow in a straight line, but through contradiction. If punk failed to teach us this lesson, we are stuck.

2006

8

Dash Snow

I.

Embodying the romantic notion of the tragic hero can be good for business in fine art. It has worked for many. The bad boy status, the outsider, the person who through a prodigious intake of hard narcotics and the frottage with petty- and non-petty criminals can bring about the cult of personality and the general foggy mystique of titillating critical attacks that the bourgeois art-buyers and gallery-walkers find so adorable, as the chosen artist pukes a bit of hi-res grit in the area designated for such in the salon.

This is of immense usefulness in bringing layered strands of self-righteousness to the particular elitist bouquet of betterment and insight that is the resounding answer to the "what purpose art" in the midst of affluent boredom. Upper middle class people love to be yelled at by outsiders and bohemians. The cozy feeling that the privileged crave repeatedly, and that the fierce, rugged and properly self-destructive individualist delivers through art/film/music/literature, well documented in, oh, Martial or Procopius or Petronius or Cato, seems to be an evergreen of the human condition. The aspirational middle class needs its howling critics like the box of rich artisanal chocolates demands a subsequent glass of ice water followed by a cordial. And as this is 2009, the louder and more anguished the howl, the tastier the bitter flavour of the digestif. The art buyer is a savvy customer tho', and has a list of demands that the artist needs to fulfill before he/she is invited to the salon at their classic 9 on lower 5th in order to add a bit of exotic yellow bile to the pattern of their Ladik Medallion: Heroin? Check. Tattoos outlandish yet within tradition? Check. Overt flaunting of subject-matters most private? Double-check. Teeth sharpened, yet sanitary to bite the feeding hand? Yes. Check.

In celebrity culture, in blogging, in snarky blog-comment postings, in the rapidly diminishing distance between street art and Madison Avenue, pubertal in-jokes and international art expos, shooting up and the discipline of the un-wanting void, there lies a heat death.

The possible final state of the solipsist universe, in which life has run down to a state of no thermodynamic free energy left to sustain motion, activity or life. This is what the bohemian artist craves, his (black bile) digestif following the Little Debbie snack cake. Nietzsche speaks of the last man, whose gaze at the wreckage of humanity brings the deep-rooted desire to be alone, and be empowered in the realization that any respite of humanist thought, ethics, systems of morality will live and die with him. Enter junk: the last man cannot realize that the two year old child in front of him, the blood of his blood, disproves those very ideas, not when crying for Mercury, but when demanding of a diaper change. The call for oblivion superceded the insight that the art execution of the man child can never compete with the artistic endeavor and primary art experiences of your own child. It is very sad that he didn't know this.

II.

And before the body has grown cold, or been autopsied, or cremated, while a legion of the acquaintances of the artist/cadaver or myth/legacy are going crazy Lower Broadway-style on-line, alternating between snarky comments about Dash's privilege, counter-snarky missives about how *real* he was, and how *real* his art *is*, or counter-counter-snark about romantic heroes (Basquiat and Shelley were among the first names to be dropped, Basquiat was mis-spelled), or counter-counter-counter snark about the hideous irresponsibility of shooting heroin when you are the parent of a small child, or (horror of horrors) the impotent howlings of the truly spiritually bankrupt; the contextualizing of the self within the sanctified realm of the dearly departed martyr. And over there is all his art: the extraordinary masterpieces that are his collages, his xeroxed artists books, his maddeningly brilliant polaroids. Shelley's "Adonais," I promise you the delivery of such, but here in these home-made tomes, Dash has written only about Dash where Shelley wrote about John Keats:

Our Adonais has drunk poison - oh!
What deaf and viperous murderer could crown
Life's early cup with such a draught of woe?
The nameless worm would now itself disown:
It felt, yet could escape, the magic tone
Whose prelude held all envy, hate and wrong,
But what was howling in one breast alone,
Silent with expectation of the song,
Whose master's hand is cold, whose silver lyre unstrung.

The mechanics of the lonely death of a wretched heart can be expressed. In the artist's books of Dash Snow you can repeatedly recognize a narrative that responds to the human condition with bafflement, to existential despair with a resounding Totlachen, to the ritualized insult of medial language with the Burroughs/Isidore Isou-like brave brevity of a dyslexic Pan chomping at the din of shmucks, and (yes) spritzing cum and glitter on the front page of the bastion of the spectacular that is the *NY Post*.

"People are just too super-conscious of every creative move made in their lives of infinite possibilities to do something outside of all contexts and just a simple expression of something with no real ramifications, at least none that the creator consciously put there." — Lester Bangs 1971

III.

Judging the work of Snow on the basis of his public persona is identical to looking at a picture of a dog taking a crap, finding merit in the act or the end product only after you've found out that the dog belongs to Brad Pitt. The cop-out of making the artist *be* the art is one of the hollowest and clangiest tones of how the empty barrel of celebrity culture is informing our perception of art and artists. The old petit-bourgeois cliché of confusing the working class with the criminal class, idealizing hooligans, infusing dissolved moral values with hipness is rarely as clear as in how the mutuality of judgment of the work and the person who executes said work has become blatant and everyday as instantaneous medial blitzkrieg demands the snark, demands the rumours, demands the personal tragedies. In *Beyond Good and Evil* Nietzsche discusses the Don Juan of knowledge, who doesn't love the things he knows, but has spirit and appetite for the chase and intrigues of knowledge. Ultimately, he is in the position where there is no knowledge left to hunt but the absolutely detrimental. Snow's transforming of everyday ephemera at its best is an inverted mimic of the idea of signal to noise ratio that William Gibson mentions in *Spook Country* talking about early modern Europe. A hierarchy of top-down signal dissemination, in an era lacking tech, imposing a near disastrous ratio, the noise of heresy constantly threatening to drown out Rome. This is what Dash Snow's collages do: the noise drowns out the medial din. Détournement is certainly the perfect act for the lazy and stoned intellectual: It gives him/her the ability to lift large chunks of text/images created by other people, incorporating it into the work, and claiming that this act in itself is more significant than coming up with original material. Than getting high. But with Dash Snow, the sense of the derive, the drifting, and the subsequent saplings he takes from our garden of earthly delights during said drift, brings about a potent headiness that is always a dead giveaway that the Situationists were artists and made art. Obviously, there can be no Situationist art, only a Situationist use of art. A détournement of pre-existing material is a Situationist act, the end result is not. If Dash hadn't died, this work in front of me would have constituted his juvenilia, and now that is all there is.

IV.

Dash was born in 1981. I remember the year well. Black Flag's LP *Damaged* was released, *Evil Dead* came out, I mastered the Ollie and read *Clans of the Alphane Moon*. All the matters of futurity that we now take for granted hadn't yet infused us in their myriads of disappointing ways. We had yet to be slowly overtaken by the wholly hideous notion that the Rapture had already come to pass, and we were the ones left behind. Or for that matter, that history had ended, it was after the end of time, and our maker had just not bothered to tell us. Hence the lack of direction, lack of rudder, no one posted as a look-out to warn us of icebergs and computer viruses. No one to tell us that maybe all politicians are demons, even the smooth and suave black ones, and that alienated consumption does not function as betterment for a future unlikely to bother with happening. And that the dress we just bought to wear at a garden party to be attended in the not too distant future, in its projection on the frontal lobe has already reached totality. And the Sad Clown of Death (who works in mid-management for a mid-sized marketing company that grew out of a failed dot.com) spends the hours after his workaday, but before the cocktail meet and greet, peeling original and authentic Dash Snow street art off of the walls of Bowery's einstürzende neubauten. The prizes are brought home, and he grants the archangel Gabriel a blissful slice of covert sanctimonious thought that he hadn't sold any of his duplicates prematurely, but can now sell these relics online where they can become potent totems for hipster shrines.

V.

To muster up the emotional energy to think about what is concealed behind the branded veils of the passing of the baton in the relay race of hip these days feels like beating egg whites to a froth with a coke spoon for a whisk. Chinese whispers: coded anointments and the perpetual deathwish attempt to arrive at the pearly gates with an immaculate pedigree and score-cards of code. The nervous waltz of a Rivington Arms opening, where jockeying and positioning is as attuned to an inner radar and sense of etiquette as the court of the sun king, or the inner circles of Ali in the years following the death of Mohammed. Codified behavior, this social pecking order derived from mystical sources, the cool and the credibility, and the fear, the fear and the teaching of the fear: Those who have it, don't know how to keep it, and are afraid. Those who don't have it, don't know how to get it, and are afraid. Art-world insiders, consumers, artists in mid-aspiration, artists whose names once shone like beacons but now are dimmed, scenesters, musicians, the people who like to see pictures of themselves in websites and magazines, perennially contextualizing themselves with the ones who actually do something: New York City's strip-miners of time, precious time, all emulating the ritualized conduct of the high school popularity contest, now orchestrated and staged as an abject counterpoint to the phony saccharine world that rejected them, and that they had to escape from, arriving at this graceful state of amoral fabulousness. It is easy to be seduced by these burlesques. The civil-war reenactment of high school cliques that are laughed at as a brightly lit example of the phony bullshit of café society, the world of fine art professionals and their haute-bourgeoisie customers must be different from all this somehow as we are their mirrour that flatters not and as we may take their money, but they sure can't take our soul. A jeans commercial or some fashion photography is a great way to pay the rent, as well as a means of subverting the system from inside. All the cool artists sold out. When Hieronymus Bosch painted those triptychs, he had actually been hired by Beelzebub to re-brand Hell. David Widgery writes about the cool of 1960's London, around people like the Rolling Stones and their entourage, where people could be dying and no one would stop to enquire why. Egotistical, pretty, bright young people, mostly on the make in some form, treating each other fairly unscrupulously. The people who suffered were not this layer but those who hung on to the myths and ended up in the squalid rat-infested squat shooting up. It was more like the sort of millennial movements that emerged in the English Civil War: somehow simply by the power of thought you can transcend material needs. But that is what comes from the rich; you ignore your own actual privileges, but you generalize from the vantage point of having them, maybe something like a westernized but no less destructive version of hikikomori, the Japanese-identified social withdrawal syndrome of single males. No one suffers like white middle class artists, because it is all in their heads. Their lives are privileged, and the true gnarl of day-to-day lives of poverty, ill health and the daily hardships of ghetto life need to be self-generated in order to create the inspiration that will result in art of a sufficiently potent caliber. One turns one's attention to the enemy within, moves to an inner ghetto, and quite oftenly commences the consumption of hard drugs, as the soci-economical life of the junkie is the most immediately swift means to arrive at the day-by-day hardships of life in the projects, the ghetto, the war zone. A gesamtkunstwerk.

An inner landscape that looks like feels like seems like the Gaza Strip. Where scavenging for drug money is emotionally identical to scurrying for fire wood or begging for drinking water. At a certain age, this strife towards a picaresque of addict picturesque (which has been described to its pinnacle in Thomas De Quincey's <u>Diary of an English Opium Eater)</u> feels so very meaningful, and is so romantic that for the disenfranchised white middle class youth, it is a flirtation of almost religious intensity and necessity. Usually designated for ones college years, and to be abandoned either immediately upon graduation of before one turns 30 whence one can then commence to reference to ones lost years as picturesque and splendid ruins that adds to the overall quality and glory of the scenically splendorous view from the outlook.

Once the baggage attached to the *Vice Magazine/National Enquirer* narrative of the life story of Dash Snow gets lost in time, like dried tears if you will, eyes will still behold his work, not knowing whether he had stayed at Gagosian's beach house or gotten high with a Rothschild or a Getty or both. Not seeing his photograph in a glossy magazine prior to eyeballing the work. And work it was, heaps and hoards and masses of it. Quality work. Work that can be perused outside of the cult of personality. But it could also go the opposite (shitty) way.

Us westerners in recent time have accomplished the ultimate mastery of the Tibetan concept of celebrity as Tulpa, the celebrity self as having a life of its own, and how it can under the right circumstances indefinitely survive the death of its subject. Collectors as mere armchair quarterbacks of life, gorging on thrills of lurid titillations, reading the life of Dash Snow, its romantic squalor, in the work as it hangs on the wall of the hallway, of the study, in the gallery, in the Hamptons, at the Thurmans is evermore the mirrour which flatters not, reflecting our collective emptiness, as a huge neon-sign of a pointing accusatory finger is strapped on the biggest bottle-rocket money can buy, aimed directly at the scenesters and gallerists and friends and peripherals who have the delusional judgment of interpreting Dash Snow's art through his life or his life through his art.

VI.

Dash Snow sprung his well-informed box-trap, and a public persona mirroring Michael Jackson was seen stepping out all over New York City: Page Six, *Vanity Fair*, *The Observer*, Gawker and Trousersnake. A façade of imperfections: crime, drugs, vandalism, juvie-hall, irresponsibility. Behind that façade, an enormous amount of work is being created. Books are published, exhibits are staged. If the artist is a celebrity-obsessed faggot that goes to every opening or a fucked up rich-kid junkie getting famous by piggy-backing his famous family, then where does all this work come from? Who does it? The junkie? The faggot? Is there a difference between the façade and its content? Can it be interpreted through the artwork? Interviews? The photographs? The bacchanalia? The hebephrenic schizophrenia of Snow's performances with Colen? Was it all "silly" or "childish" behavior? Was it all affectations? Dash Snow certainly knew that intelligence is advertising turned inside out. Secrets are cool. The very root of cool. A most marketable commodity certainly, but also like Fred Vermorel suggested, how to paint your subjectivity in the codes of culture and foment an insurrection of like-minded solitudes. Spontaneous consent, the hegemony that controls the taste, the means of controlling ideology or what is called taste.

70

When Holbein's *Dance of Death* came to be issued, five years before Holbein succumbed to the plague, it was initially published anonymously, as its indictment of the Catholic Church was severe. I dare say that Dash, at his best, is indicting his audience with a severity of similar strength, and that as collective emptors, we better have ourselves pretty damn caveated, or else avert our gaze from his unleashed Id and Superego as it stares down his blood-circles of privilege, stares down his fame-merchants and stares down the verysame parasites who are blogging themselves brightly purple with fawning acclaim as the eversame were cursed by the man mere weeks before. Now with death no longer the great equalizer, but instead where the hollow dried-up husk of existence gets replaced by iconography and façade, the cargo cult is aptly on the rise in the perennial death-trip neighborhoods of large cities where the tyranny of the new is the tyranny of the old and the sun shone lacking alternative upon the eversame. But let us remember our Shelley, let us remember our Bangs, and let us remember Dash Snow, let us react to his work, to his short and cumbersome life.

> *O gentle child, beautiful as thou wert,*
> *Why didst thou leave the trodden paths of men*
> *Too soon, and with weak hands though mighty heart*
> *Dare the unpastur'd dragon in his den?*
> *Defenceless as thou wert, oh, where was then*
> *Wisdom the mirror'd shield, or scorn the spear?*
> *Or hadst thou waited the full cycle, when*
> *Thy spirit should have fill'd its crescent sphere,*
> *The monsters of life's waste had fled from thee like deer.*

2009

9

Mario Panciera's *45 Revolutions*: A Punk Anatomy of Melancholy

Mario's homeboy Piero Camporesi[1] speaks in his book *The Anatomy of the Senses* about the *dreaded desire to study* as a not uncommon problem among the bourgeois youth of the 16th and 17th century in Northern Italy. Where the demands and expectations hovering over the heads of these kids, and the knowledge of the travails and sacrifices that their parents had gone through in order for them to receive their coveted slot at the university of, say, Bologna (where Camporesi was professor of history up until his, uh, timely death[2]) would drive these unfortunate youngsters to study until they collapsed from exhaustion and in some instances died. Thank God we still have Mario Panciera with us. He has for more than a quarter of a century suffered from this malaise vis-à-vis punk rock.

Where most shmoes and shmo-ettes remove themselves forcefully from the cartoon rebellion of their white middle class teenage years, some of us simply can not permanently leave for the inferior world of the squares: How does one make a life in a world dominated by chartered accountancy, play dates, Bermuda shorts and the worship of shmengies, whilst one's very soul reverberates from those handfuls of art experiences that split our minds wide open during those formative adolescent years? When Mario Panciera went to a bunch of gigs at the Roxy in 1977 as a receptive and (no doubt) starry-eyed teen, the stage was set for a life-long obsession with the mighty rock that had punked him. These obsessions, for us males, lacking in the ability to breast-feed or the commencement of multiple orgasms[3], can often lead us down the path of collecting, with its implications of mastery of a narrowly defined universe and therefore immortality.

---

1 This historian specializing in the culture, eats, dreams and desires of common Italian 17th century folk is never less than a fascinating read. Start with Anatomy of the Senses or The Magic Harvest.

2 His students envied and/or feared him. His exams were legendary monstrosities where approximately 3 out of every 4 students would fail. Students would assume fake names to avoid ending up in his class since the lottery betwixt the three history professors was divided alphabetically.

3 Rumor has it that Sting (notable in this book only for his bass playing on the god-awful Radio Actors 45) has, through rigorous yoga, started to lactate.

Not to mention how fun it is to surround yourself with tonsa cool goodies that you, yourself and you have hunted and gathered for in all four corners of the world and/or Ebay. Especially true all this, as a means of escapist flights of fancy from the world we inhabit, the world of chartered accountancy and Bermuda shorts breathes down our collective necks in a way less than pleasant. The similarities in how yoga breathing and alphabetical filing of rare punk 45s minimizes panic attacks are legion.

To know as much as possible about a narrow field is a grand tradition of Western thought: Mario, in the noble manner of say, Ernst Jünger (insects), John Cage (mushrooms) and William Gibson (rare wrist-watches), is a true expert in a field that to the casual observer is quite far removed from his generally acknowledged substantial talent as a composer of modern symphonic music. But one hand does wash the other. The man who is passionate enough to follow the four winds of the world in a relentless pursuit of the alternate picture sleeve for The Opus' "The Atrocity" will bring that passion with him wherever those winds will take him, and to whatever pastime or discipline he chooses. Baking bread, fixing cars or planting perennials, it is all the same.

As a true lover of 70's punk, I rate the 17th century as the very pinnacle of western thought and expression: the age of enlightenment, when all the sciences and disciplines co-existed peacefully with myth, legend and dreams, perfectly mirrors the early days of punk rock. The time where this movement truly existed on the fringe, in the margins, and where its singular outsider status created its own aesthetic worth, in fact, made it all up as they went along, was a time when this was in no way a mass culture. The colorful shorts of SoCal whoopee-cushion punk was decades away, and people from all walks of life (as long as they were white and middle class) made the very nostrils of their art school teacher flare in irritation as they subverted up a storm with swastikas and stenciled clothing, not to mention barely tuned fuzztone guitar. There were no rules within a musical field that embraced anyone from Throbbing Gristle to Television. New ideas met old, exited stage left, sliced up some bread, silk-screened the face of Gottlob Frege thereupon to finally chew it up and puke it out on the stage of CBGB or the 100 Club.

Mario's editorial decision of making December 31st, 1979 the cut-off for inclusion into this volume, is at face value as arbitrary as all get, but so is a century, so is a decade. The phrases we use daily as yardsticks and definers are by their nature, arbitrary and subtle, not to say vague. There are many records described within this volume that are no more punk with a capitol unk than your Uncle Fred. Bands that would've at the time been absolutely mortified to be affiliated with the schmutzed and safety-pinned sons and daughters of hair-dye. Bands where the music cozies up to Jim Croce or Dire Straits with more familiarity than they would ever have with Crocus Behemoth or Frankie Fix. Yet, their private press origin and their (unaware) side-step from the imperialist (hot-cha-cha!) record business makes their inclusion in this book much more valid than, oh, say, the fucking Dead Boys.[4]

The more I read about punk rock, the more convinced I am that, like the birth of many-a movement, it did not happen in a linear fashion, nor did it happen in one single place at one point in time. It happened, simultaneously, all over the world, and the complicated webwork of ideas feeding ideas sucking blood from ideas ripping off ideas can not be compressed into a tidy little package no matter how we try. And why would we try?

We shouldn't try. Life is not a Harry Stephen Keeler[5] novel. It does not all fit in. The contents of this book, and the ungodly, awe-inspiring scholarly undertaking of Mario is here, not to explain what happened, but as a magnificent cabinet of wonders and curiosities that will smitten and enthuse generations to come. How cool is that?

2003

---

4 You know there is no difference between the Dead Boys and Judas Priest.

5 Monstrous, probably insane, Chicago author of webwork novels, active during the first half of the 20th century. A charitable person would describe his books as coincidence-porn. Sample plot: A dwarf dressed up as an infant hovering in an autogyro over a perfectly manicured cricket lawn murders some guy. Sample novel title: The Skull of the Waltzing Clown. He is the business for fans of unintentional surrealism, and aren't we all?

10

This is Truly a Cabinet of Curiosities

I.

In the wake of internet sites where you can pilfer among the stuff of hundreds of thousands, the search words you command will lead to what you locate, which in turn means that what you find and purchase and what becomes your punk rock history hoard curates itself through your choices (the snail asks itself was it good for you? did you orgasm?). The blaze of the first Ramones album and the tabula rasa of its stance and aggro is no less difficult to grasp in April of 2011, 35 years after its release. Works of art outside of time shake us up, and 20/20 historian hind-legs hindsight does not take away from the visceral experience. It is a pure hit of a white light/white heat sugar blast, and as the drug/candy reference is surgically extracted, in its place is a comparison to Siegfried's Death March or West End Blues or Mississippi John Hurt's "Stag-O-Lee Blues," or even, notwithstanding the 1976 A&R department, the 1976 publicity department and the 1976 label and management's escalated hopes/thoughts that what they were hoisting onto the turntables of a reluctant audience was the 1910 Fruitgum Company with Springsteen's balls. It all didn't matter as these very same professionals midwifed great art for the wrong reasons, a consistent specialty of the record business. The Stooges were signed for Iggy's Morrisonesque croon, not to mention his Morrisonesque ability to make them swoon. The Velvet Underground got their record deal as the unpalatable *artistic* filling that was needed for the Warhol pop-art sugar cookie not to merely taste of artificial banana (a dick joke lifted from Ed Sanders/Fugs), but to provide a touch of bitter flavors and humours necessary to titillate the jaded palate of the pop consumer. Warhol as a brilliant savant recognized the marketplace for a *o-tempora-o-mores-non-compos-mentis* art-mass market multiple, and so did Verve Records. After hearing the sublime sturm und drang of the first pass at the album, a house producer was brought in to book-end the frenzied screech with two slickly produced aquarian feel-good ballads. A second spoonful of sugar helped the medicine go down. And in 1972, a veritable school of record biz fishies thought that the New York Dolls were going to sell a ton of records and that Kiss and Aerosmith ain't would sell any. Any cultural theory of the sublime would probably hold water: Johnny Thunders guitar-lines are as graceful and jagged as any surviving semi-ruinous roman aqueduct, the sub-Stones-slop of the mighty racket mirror the American teen punk bands circa 65/66, and the image was rampant omni-sexual *Them*-doom: all-commentary on those brilliant Manhattan drag-queens who provided the blue-print for any aesthetic or emotional statement of outsiderdom and the perennial glamour of the gutter. As an inverted stratified value statement and/or jest appears in the critical acclaim of artists who had a hard time paying the rent, not to mention the counter-point of the mega-successful artist consumed by bitterness that he/she completely lack in pop culture street (blog) credibility, the notion of what punk *became* as a signifier and yard-stick is still a maze and a riddle, and amen to that. The history of the punk aesthetic can not be told, only shown, and if the envelope needs to shift its placement further, remember the immortal words of Marco Pironi, who with maximum hindsight super-power came to exclaim that punk never did happen.

II.

The jejune of the 75 punk books I have read in the past year will not be further addressed, as Flann O'Brien said in *At Swim Two Birds* that fighting in front of strangers is the height of vulgarity. It may also be noted that if you give the same answer to all questions the perception is either of infinite wisdom or infinite ignorance. Stating "punk is dada" with a loud voice, as one sips a cappuccino, spilling the slightest bit of foamy milk on the black turtleneck, might not be that dramatic a statement anymore: in fact, people sipping Watney's Red Barrel, draped in a Manchester City shirt, will glance over and yawn, thinking what you just said was a given, a cliché, a pedestrian platitude so populist as to have lost its meaning as they reach for their darts. But don't let it stop you: Punk is Dada.

The moustachioed presenter of I think it was *Old Grey Whistle Test* glanced smirkingly into the camera and intoned toff-nosedly "Mock Rock" after a performance of the New York Dolls on said show. As if that is a bad thing! The Dolls crossing the line drawn between un-aware and self-aware rock parody. Or maybe balancing on it?

Was PJ Proby self-parodic? Screaming Lord Sutch? Little Richard? Does it matter at all? What does "mock-rock" mean? That the band are making fun of the rock & roll ritual and formula as they embrace it? That rock should be taken more seriously?

We must remember that all these glam bands existed far-removed from the print-media-sanctioned musics of the first half of the seventies. The British music weeklies dismissed them as teeny-bopper crap while embracing Peter Hamill, Gentle Giant, Gong and Caravan. The similarly flavored retro-moves of the pub rock scene which followed glam as parallel diaspora received instant cred from the journos, where instant derision was what you got if you chose to play your fifties-retro-rock moves dressed in glittery pantaloons and platforms instead of flatcaps, 501's and work-boots. Iron Virgin's or the NY Dolls' or The Sweet's musical kinship to, oh, Ducks Deluxe is uncanny certainly, and since neither band really sold any records or gathered much notoriety beyond us record collectors means that with a 35+ year 20/20 hindsight we can proudly and loudly state that *both* glam rock and pub rock were counter-reactive to hippie rock and progressive rock and LA session-hack country rock and soft rock and all that festering shmaltz that truly ruled the musical everyday. But the irony is that record collectors and teeny-boppers actually indulged in the same basic musical language circa 1974 or so. The Fifties rock revival of the early 1970's brought about some strange and mighty changes in popular culture, and as per usual, the driving force behind this spectacular change were the consumption habits of the aspirational lower middle class. In the years following the war, with the immense wealth resulting from the division of the spoils by the USA and Great Britain, these glorious side-effects of war contracting agreements (still in place to this day) led to an aspirational self-indulgence from class stratas that previously had been too preoccupied with everyday survival to pursue the improvement of societal status, and the materials that would provide such. This was how the pop culture collectible was born. The re-gathering of totem-objects of childhood, or sometimes, the acquisition of items your parents wouldn't buy for you, or items that your family couldn't afford, or for that matter, articles of clothing they couldn't afford. All this adding to the fabric that drapes the soul of the kidult, a brand new marketing concept that saw its earliest inception in the rock & roll revival of the early 1970's. I have bitched about the entitlement of the baby boomers elsewhere, and sometimes in bars, but at least the infantile regression of the seventies fifties nostalgia brought about some amazing and unlikely pop-culture regurgitation.

III.

It isn't necessarily stuff that is any good, but I am not too sure that we would have had Epitaph or the White Stripes or Emo/Screamo or the Warped Tour if wasn't for what the pre-punk punks set in motion. The trickle-down of white middle-class self-starter culture into the myriad of cartoon rebellion flavors of 2007 has as its genesis some pretty damn good ideas. Notwithstanding that the music that has resulted from them being a bit shit, the potency of the grassroots concepts that now have reverberated for a few decades is pure sunny goodness:

The anyone-can-do-it ethos of the locally produced 45, the growth and establishing of the American independent touring circuit (built from the ground up by the SST/Dischord/Touch&Go axis of headshave),Gem's US import of independently released punk records in the 1970's and 1980's, Systematic's and Dutch East India's national distribution of any American independently released record in the 1980's, these are among the building blocks that have taken us to the national emo/punk/metal/screamo network that unites tens of thousands of Cheap Monday-draped fans with their likewise sad-panted idols. Bands that can sell out a thousand-seater venue without having a record out. Bands that you and me have never heard of. Self-starter culture for the proverbial kids, it really is too bad that the music is no good. Or maybe it is good that I can't find any quality in these bands. They most certainly aren't for me, and the difference between me as the self-professed hepcat version of parental fuddy-duddy and the dude in 1966 who fought in WW2 wanting to strangle his son and his good for nothing friends in their band, the One Way Street, making a unholy racket in his garage are naturally nil, null and void.

An uncomfortable truth as per the parallels between Emo and Garage Punk sits in the room as a bright pink elephant complete with a gold-plated albatross around its neck: Pre-psych sixties garage bands were threatened by a looming war, by the draft, by a future of uncertain fiscal empowerment and were informed by a sense of meaninglessness as far as their lives in suburbia were concerned. They formed bands, they wrote three chord songs, they bitched about girls, they bragged, they whined about their powerlessness. And the music ruled. Far be it from me to locate bands that fit within the emo parameters, executing something along the lines of "The Rat's Revenge" and then distributing it to their brethren and sisthren with geometrically challenged coiffeurs on Facebook.

But remember your Asger Jorn next time you're forcing your sister's children to listen to the Misfits: every cartoon rebellion grows old and dies without seeing its successors, because succession doesn't follow in a straight line, but through contradiction, and nowadays through contradiction that is oddly tweaked within a recognizable historical context.

Or maybe I ain't looking hard enough, or in the right place, or maybe I don't even know what I am looking for, but that is a great privilege of age. A lot of what we do as we are immersed in the cartoon rebellion of youth is making gestures, and that is all right. Rock can get you laid, and I think that Ernst Jünger would approve if I maintain that the Grains of Sand, the Alarm Clocks or the Standells can make us for a moment step outside of time. When that legion of super-dusted salary-men start slam-dancing to "Should I Stay Or Should I Go" in the sports bar where you took shelter from the rain, don't frown, throw them a spiritual bone instead. Throw one to the emo kids, they might fetch and go cover "The Rat's Revenge."

2007

11

A Smile on Your Lips, a Song in Your Heart and a Skull in Your Pocket: What on Earth is Wrong with all Those Music Blogs?

I'd like to toss off my personal top ten of problematic problems filled with issues that commence from reading music blogs. *Nota bene*: I use the term "tossed off" as it felt very apropos.

I.

Most bloggers get lost. The act of blogging means that you are lost.

II.

If the kids of the Noughts don't know that they are alienated, does that mean that they aren't alienated?

III.

Name-checking the greats does not affiliate you with said greats, no matter what Google or Wikipedia say.

IV.

The pose of the cynic in rock & roll fandom is ultimately a sham: this is an emotional landscape littered with bleeding hearts, aching loins and throbbing skulls.

V.

There is no discernable difference between neo-acid-folk and the token dorm hippie moping tunelessly.

VI.

Albert Camus' *The Myth of Sisyphus* was written about the poor man who is the guitar tech for Sonic Youth on tour, preparing 30 differently tuned electric guitars that sound identical.

VII.

Current independent underground hip hop records celebrated for their collage techniques and psychedelic layering of sound are more like the 80's/90's Chicago Wax Trax scene than anyone would like to admit.

VIII.

The bearded men that spend thousands of dollars in the quest for the rarest and funkiest 45s rarely dance and are rarely able to get ladies to sleep with them. Hence, they will rarely experience what the musical term originated from with the one exception being their sartorial standards.

IX.

Punk rock legends carrying the curse of having been at the right place at the right time up the crowded hill, rolling their most memorable tune in front of them only to watch it roll back down on the other side, hoping to die before they get older older older.

X.

The surreal, Breton-esque habit of vitriolic denouncing of blog-comrades as soon as the merits of musical choice do not completely overlap makes one feel relieved that these people never will enjoy any real public power or influence.

(---)

At this point for me, it is very difficult to read any music writing that isn't in fanzines. This is problematic, since fanzines are close to obsolete, and have been replaced by music blogs. Music blogs are very difficult to read. I spend a lot of time chasing down old rock fanzines. Really old. From the days before punk really was punk. How hard it used to be to find out about stuff. Here again! The rock t-shirt metaphor: I am old enough to remember how the spotting, three towns away, of a dude wearing a Ramones t-shirt was enough to fuel a couple of dozen of telephone calls, or for that matter, if you saw someone in a Cramps shirt at a show, you immediately struck up a conversation. I will readily admit that these are romantic notions of a grass roots culture that has since demised, demised out of necessity, probably. The nature of social reality and the means to its transformation are not to be found in the study of power, but in a long clear look at the seemingly trivial gestures and accents of ordinary experience. And this is why rock fanzines of the pre-punk era are important and why I love them.

Here are ten favorites:

Rollin' Rock

This fascinating read provides an ever-deepening context for not only pre-punk rock fandom, but it also shows that the Cramps or *Kicks Magazine* or Mad Mike of Moldies fame didn't come from a vacuum at all. This raging tough-fifties rock & roll anti-hippie 'zine had its roots in collectors/dealers set lists, which was how rare records were bought + sold + traded in the days before Ebay. Lists of records for sale intermingle with rants about obscure rockabilly artists, reprints of rare clippings from 50's print media, berserk Tim Warren-esque illustrations, and hilarious put-downs of the squares of the day.

I quote from the back cover: *"Have you had it with Bobby Sherman, Cat Stevens, James Taylor, The Carpenters, Crosby, Stills & Nash, Chicago??? Are you sick and tired of all these sex-less, whitewashed, psychedelic pop-shit groups???? ...if so, why doncha subscribe to* Rollin' Rock Magazine *and dig some of that wild, crazy, juicy, greasy, all-American rock and roll music!!!!!"* Kicks *before* Kicks *in 1971!*

Jamz

The late n' great Alan Betrock published an absolutely great rock fanzine. One can utilize some different methods reading and processing the texts in these crumbling mimeographed tomes: marveling at the word-smithery of Meltzer or Sanders, basking in the historiocity of reading contemporary accounts of the release of records and the performances of concerts that years later have become pure legend or myth. But with Alan Betrock's zine, you can also dig in from a perspective of pure consumer guidance: he was a terrific, enthusiastic writer, with that rare ability to make you enthuse alongside with him, and acquire that fevered need to hear the sounds that he is writing about. This is what bloggers should aspire to in my book: the name-calling and swagger and constipated-tough-guy tactics prevailing should be delegated to something else. Maybe it could be called rocksnarkdom instead of rockfandom?

Denim Delinquent

How hip were these guys? Well: They published a frothing anti-Patti Smith statement already in the summer of 1976! *Denim Delinquent* is a fantastic read: Astute assessments and character assassinations of a variety of rock's sacred cows *without* the benefit of 20/20 hindsight. Hepcats, I tell you, hepcats!

New Haven Rock Press

I have smothered the steak of rock & roll history with a continuous sprinkling of the minced spring onions of factoids elsewhere in pursuit of the occult lore of the pre-punk years, with the rhapsodic featured gnosis of punkage being that it *is* de facto fanzine music, and that it *didn't* have a starting date, and as I glance at the crumbling crutons of arcana that is the salted- and peppered- type on the mimeographed sheets of romaine lettuce in this here caesar salad of rock history, I hold the anchovies of pre-punk fact along the Kyocera chopping knife of deduction, illuminated by the inclusion in this here kickass (and somewhat neglected) zine' by such respectable anti-hippie pure punk statements such as Meltzer's glorious feature on Hippies In Jello ((quite the dish./Tired Ed.)), the "How To Unfold the Rolling Stone" collage, the fake "Ralph Gleason is Dead" memorandum or hilarious and punked out features on the Winos and the NY Dolls.

Brain Damage

This barrage of mesmerizing in-joke froth and Python's-with-surgically-removed-bullshit-detector-art attack has me levitating in the rec room, all aglow, wondering if this isn't the right time to crack open a bottle of 1970 Baron de Pichon, or maybe my own skull. This January 1974 one-shot by Metal Mike Saunders and Gene Sculatti reaches positively Olympian or maybe Teenage Wastelandian levels of mirth-mixed obnoxiousness. The fake letter page is amazing with ultra-vicious parodies of every BNF circa 1974. I think I'll quote the fake Lester Bangs letter:

"Dear WTTS, Just received the first 43 issues of Who Took The Shelves, *and I had to let you know how excited I am. Your mag sure does fill a void, not only in being a magazine by and for methed-up lunatics like me, but in being chock full of some of the most interesting pornography on the scene today... by any chance would you be interested in a 72-page article on Question Mark & The Mysterians?"*
– Lester Bangs El Cajon CA

Nix On Pix

Punk Rock was already in use as a term to discuss mid-sixties American teenage rock bands by 1969/1970. Ho-de-hum from the peewee gallery who knew that already. Well: It is important to point this out once in a while, we gotta note that people writing for rock fanzines during the first half of the seventies would listen to current bands from the aesthetic parameters of sixties punk, and judge the merit of given bands from this point of view, from this particular rose-tint of google-eyed goggles. This is certainly not the only catalyst for the fanzine-rock/ proto-punk bands that started showing up 73/74/75, with subsequent records being released, but it certainly was one of them. As each issue of *Nix On Pix* is choc-full of punk rock, whether the date it is postmarked reads 1972 or 1975, the modern/2008 reader (me!) can't help but reverberate in bafflement how far the reach of these holy men of taste-making actually reached. Truly theirs was the voice of God as the Son of Perdition spread noxious musical fumes from FM stations and the pages of *Rolling Stone*.

Penetration

It wasn't all the USA. The UK proto-punk post-hippie semi-pro-zine *Penetration* is a fascinating example of the pre-punk narrative I hollered and hooted about in issue 26 of *Ugly Things*: as consecutive issues of Paul Welsh' brilliant zine are read, you notice how the shape of punk aesthetics to come are here found ripening like a Lincolnshire Poacher. Stooges? Check. Velvets? Check? The aggro side of pub rock? Check. Hawkwind as an outta space garage band? Double check. What adds to the general suaveness of the mag is that they also have great taste in *tough* hippies (Soft Machine, Kevin Ayers, Deviants, Henry Cow) while ignoring or dismissing douchey hippies (list too long to mention).

Rock News

And meanwhile, in Paris! I've always thought that the French have unjustifiably gotten the short end of the stick rock-cred-wise. We all know they are the only people shmucky enough to like Tom Waits, but cut 'em some slack: they can also be the acme of hep, and effortlessly so. By 1974, France had Skydog Records, the Dogs, Little Bob Story, and by next year, another answer to the perennial question of what was the first punk fanzine reared its head. Just before *Punk Magazine*, and long before *Sniffin' Glue*, this slew of six issues published by future ZE Records honcho Mechel Esteban in 1975/1976 were informed by and informed the punk scene as it was unfolding.

Future

This creation by Chesterfield King Greg Prevost can be described as the last pre-punk fanzine. The premier issue came out in early 1977, and is a masterpiece of adolescent swagger and crazed music-fanatic brou-hah-hah. inside jokes, absurd comix and one sentence hatchet job reviews intersplice with hyper-informed blasts of pure enthusiasmos about everything from the Kinks to the Residents.

Diddy Wah Diddy

To round off the list, like buttah in da sauce, I'm including issue number one of Brad Balfour's fanzine *Diddy Wah Diddy* from May of 1971. Its feature article states loudly and clearly: *"The punkoid rocker of the seventies is merely the fifties greaser in drag."* Our beloved Japanese hardcore band of yore, Gism, were inaccurate when they stated "Punks Is Hippies" on record and on t-shirt circa mid-1980's. "Punks Is Greasers." Malcolm McLaren wouldn't have to have changed the name of the shop and punks and rockers didn't have to fight.

I'd like to commence my shadow-boxing of the soap-box, hopefully with some moxie. Fanzines as stapled objects are more or less dead. There are civil-war re-enactors publishing Xeroxed tomes all over town, usually the same people who have now made the cassette the new 78 of hipster cache. This is evermore a death rattle. Fanzines are dead, replaced by blogs. Dead like set sale record lists, replaced by Ebay. So: what has been lost, is the mystery of finding rare music and locating the like-minded, what has been gained, is ways to find rare music, and to locate the like-minded. The difference is that all of this is now done without all the mystery. Which is better? If you are old, it is the old way. The romantic notion of scarcity, of the sacred quest for the holy punk record, of not really knowing if you'd ever even get to hear a copy of the Screamin' Mee-Mees *Live in the Basement* EP. Every visit to the local second hand record shop was a quest, but with guaranteed results. If you dug around long enough, you'd find something you'd dig. The mail order rare record catalogue was an event, and the fevered frenzy of not knowing whether the best stuff on Paul Major's or Chuck Warner's set list had sold before you got your order in was in many ways a superior adrenaline rush to the instant gratification (or not!) of an Ebay auction win. While we always will be prevented from truly browsing, flea-market-style, on Ebay due to its inept interface, Youtube has no such problems: Youtube, warts and all, is one of the websites that most closely resembles the 10,000 square foot used vinyl emporium of yore, or the vast vinyl deposits in gigantic thrift stores throughout the rust belt. And in a way Youtube is better: You don't have to spend any money, you can immediately share your finds with your compadres, and you don't have to sustain yourself on a diet of exclusively belly-bomb grease on your hunting and gathering expeditions. Also: as a long-time collector of vanity pressings, I can honestly say that there are things available on Youtube that has exorcized any of my remaining jadedness. In an odd way, Youtube feels like it has much more to do with the spirit of pre-punk rock & roll fandom than the blogs. When you find something amazing, then you can go through the rest of the postings by the person in question, finding more amazing stuff, without having to read the epic tides of unedited logorrheic swill banged out by some doofus who'd be more appropriate at Speakers Corner in Hyde Park with a megaphone than on your computer screen just cuz you google-searched This Heat.

Blogs aren't fanzines. They are more like being cornered by a drunken fanatical fan wafting halitosis, droning on and on about what they are basing their "I'm-Right-You're-Wrong"-worldview on, and as they maintain Little Egypt's flimsiest and final veil of enthusiasm for their totem-artist of choice, what they truly like to do is to bitch about things they think suck. Bitch, bitch, bitch. Suck, suck, suck. Being published on your own blog still feels like being published, it feels *important*. Before, the limitations of the dimension of the printed page, and the workload involved with the actual production of a fanzine, was/is the best editor rock fans could have: Only the fans that had the ability to conquer their inner sloth would publish actual fanzines choc-a-bloc smeared with logorrhea slightly neutered or sharpened by re-writes and enchanted duplicators.

On the rarest of occasion, internet blog prose hoo-hah manages to pass through the tunnel and come out on the other side. I found this on some blog, and notwithstanding that I have no idea what this guy is on about, the surrealist prose is splendidly refreshing.
Can one hope for automatic record review writing?:

> *The Homosexuals(pre-[In Exile]original version, the one on newly assembled THE HOMOSEXUALS RECORD and ASTRAL GLAMOUR) are being hyped as more of ye "post-punk pioneers." True, they did seize the right moment to move past punkthrodoxy (which early tracks prove they so bad at). But not to slide those ol' enosizers out of the closet for dance class, like Go4, Joy D., etc. No, the 'mos just let it rip and trip, into twin barrels of four-eyed Nerd Power, much less anal than Elvis Costello's or Devo's. Foreskinners of current shatter-trope spewcore, of which Mars Volta might be one of the more conservative examples.(Homosex of recs are more like Freedie and the Dreamers x vulcanized lick and proto-jangle enhanced by digital x Wire-asides x Mars V. x Fountains of Wayne? As high as I can find things to count on right now.) Spirit of punkadelica outside the laws of style and cool, and kind good, once they get a no-handle on it. But after all come to think of it including poptones, ground and oops into the goo-goo, so I guess Lydon *might* or o course certainly should have approvved this,however reluctatnly, and thus it's "post-punk" after all. Well that's a relief isn't it?*[6]

6 http://thefreelancementalists.blogspot.com/2004/07/soon-after-sling-blade-became-left.html

Pure sound poetry. Worthy of the band he is writing about. A best case scenario. More often though, blog writing reminds me of Amanda McKettrick Ros. Her novel *Delina Delaney* begins with the following music/politico-blog-esque sentence:

"Have you ever visited that portion of Erin's plot that offers its sympathetic soil for the minute survey and scrutinous examination of those in political power, whose decision has wisely been the means before now of converting the stern and prejudiced, and reaching the hand of slight aid to share its strength in augmenting its agricultural richness?"

The flavor of *terribilità* that comes across in the blog-reading experience is usually along the lines of wondering what the heck the writer is on about. Friedrich Schlegel's slices of rhetorical irony also pointed the way a couple of centuries ago: where critical writing is revealing its own artifice by exposing the hand of the creator intruding the text. Music blogging isn't quite as nasty as food blogging when it comes to this. Imagine the damage Calvin Trillin has done: this exemplary and exquisite writer, through his perennial ability to incorporate his family and friends in his narratives, has brought about legions of aging indie-rockers telling us about the barbeque they ate with their girlfriend "who works in media." Certainly: great writers midwife bad writers as great musicians midwife sucky ones. The masses certainly are asses that need better glasses, but the watered down trickle-down of mass consumption where Pat Boone is the norm instead of Little Richard, or, for that matter, Ralph Gleason instead of Bangs/Meltzer, does have a silver lining: as a Carte de Tendre, fanatical music fans can gaze upon mainstream music or music writing and notice how it does not fulfill their needs, or provide them with the desired visceral roadmap through life, and therefore turn to underground rekkids and fanzines, pursuing a cultural-metaphorical demand to piss and shit in different colors. My hope is that same desire is turning people away from the blogs, and it seems like it is happening. Some luddites are even putting out fanzines.

2007

12

The Drawings of Ragnar Persson

I know Ragnar Persson's drawings as I once lived inside of them, a long time ago, in a place far, far away.

Ragnar's work reverberates with the moods and landscapes of the far north of Sweden, which is where my adolescence took place. Persson's drawings feel like the memory of a horror comic you owned when you were ten. Like how it felt to close your eyes as hard as you could while listening to *Master of Puppets* on your headphones. The permutation of adolescent fear, its tinge even in moments of abject happiness. The work contains within it the melancholy visceral fleshiness of distant dreams and memories.

Ex-pats often talk about the colors and smells of where they are from. Whether you are a transplant from the Swedish north, to the metropolis of Stockholm, or whether you leave your native country for a place far, far away, the color of the trees, the sound of the forest and the smell of the water will never leave you, and it is almost as if your very atoms rejoice whenever you return to pastures of childhood lost. I feel all this and more, when viewing Ragnar's drawings.

Childhood (as does adolescence) has a component of brutality, always. A Swedish provincial childhood more so, as I flash upon those darkest days of my own and its rickety dances of life and death: my mother would point out which barns people had shot themselves in, which lakes had seen drowning, which house façades concealed madness and grotesque unhappiness. This is gothic, grotesque, pathetic and panoramic, like grand opera narratives, like the cover images on extreme metal albums, like Ragnar's work. They are also filled with the abstract sense of wonder, sense of longing and sense of tumultuous sexual confusion of adolescence, and the drawings that all of us in our teenage incarnation scribbled in class, in coffee shops, in art class.

How disposable a given art is is already defined by its intent: Ragnar Persson's drawings, very close in my visceral read to scribbles in the notebook of the high school stoner (if that stoner had had a working

97

knowledge of illuminated manuscripts, 18th and 19th century zoological textbooks and Linne's *Botanica*), rest assured on a foundation of mortality: time runs in both directions, as the Stoic dudes pointed out, and the accumulated past is contained within the work, as the diminishing future communicates the work. Friday and Saturday night in small town Sweden, where for youth, so many things must be made to happen in such very short span of time, result in occurrences and dramas of such heightened emotional intensity that the narratives of metal, of horror movies, of romance novels, of porn are appropriate guiding lights, like living inside Opera Buffa, all emotions heightened to absolute pinnacle. This coexists with a frenetic small town creative happiness. Outsiders in rural areas and small communities find each other through a process similar to osmosis, and enjoy each other's company out of necessity. Bridging the gap and the shackles of taste and tribe in a mutuality of outsiderdom. I remember it fondly: metalheads and punks and hippies and gays and weirdos and science-fiction nerds socializing in a grand scheme alliance against the square world.

These solvent bonds of friendship didn't necessarily transcend your own particular microcosm though: if you grow up a hick in Sweden (which means growing up almost anywhere except Stockholm), and you find yourself smitten by the arts at an early age as a way of avoiding the omnipotence of sports, you are able, by the means of the lightning-speed Swedish way of cultural derivativeness, to find yourself thoroughly *informed* about the cultural ongoing of the world at large within your given field. This rang true 25 years ago as I grew up in a village in the north, and the truth rings even more so with a life contaminated by broadband internet access. Within your field, you have to trump your little friends in knowledge and connoisseurship, not in enthusiasm. Those moments of youthful levity, when art opens your mind to infinite possibilities for the first time, instead become circumspect, and a matter of *what use art* in the immensely complicated social stratifications of the life of small-town youth. Identity is everything, and your personal otherness, your outsiderdom is privilege as much as it is armour, a way of living, as much as a means of rejecting.

I remember the awkwardness of the man-children in the inner circle of black metal notoriety. What I've taken with me from the times when they crossed my path is this: whenever one of the key players would visit the record distribution company owned by my old friend, they seemed to have pumped themselves up; with hot air, with emotional steroids, with anger and righteousness and a fragile aggressive swagger that I recognize either-which-way as that of the outsider coming in. The big-city Stockholm people would never feel fear and nervous aggression in anticipation of going to a record shop, or for a chat with the distributor of their home-made cassettes and vinyls, as the charade of their artistic endeavor prohibits them from the seriousness and ridiculousness enveloped in that very fear.

The moments when the gaze of the outsider is forced to look directly in are psycho-dramas of shivering instability. The trip to the big city record shop, the journey to the big rock festival, the pub on Friday and Saturday night, and the subsequent queue outside the fast food outlet later the same night are when the troll can't keep away, when it craves closeness to the dwellings of humankind, the warmth, the song, the dance, in the midst of its knowledge of the danger involved and the impending doom for them, and the immersions cultivated as a protective coating. An instinctive understanding of Guy Debord's axiom: "There is nothing more natural than to consider everything as starting from oneself, chosen as the center of the world; one finds oneself thus capable of condemning the world without even wanting to hear its deceitful chatter."

The people who treat the pop culture landscape as yet another career choice, like an advertising agency or a marketing company, chomping at the bits in eagerness to sell their product, their self to whatever caffeine-drink brand has room in its fourth quarter budget, have never created any art of longevity. They reduce art to an ordinary social construct, like a commute to work or the remodeling of a kitchen. Luckily, the artist can observe all this, deem it not able to fulfill one's need for authenticity or emotional grounding, and become an outsider looking out. Sweden has always been full of these double-nickel-on-the-dime outsiders. Where the work is a ritualized conduct to keep people out, to keep people away, a secret handshake of outsiderdom, where only a certain select few can construe the meaning contained within, or be able to connect with the person behind the work. In Scandinavia, this seems to be a necessary survival strategy for youth, and the source of some of its most potent art. This feels like a handy counter-attack against people or institutions who have shunned you. It results in your gain of control over your dreams, as the people who are your *they* are powerless there. In your dreams began irresponsibilities. This strategy, and the resulting potency of the work can and will often be mired with dangerous nihilism, as the outsider status truly becomes a dream weapon in a society that is perceived by the outsider to be somnambulant, with the nihilist streak stemming from the subsequent notion of stratified realness, the internal otherness becomes external: the normals are worth less, they mean less, they feel less and know less. Dangerous magical thinking. One can certainly understand how to get there, and some of us spent a lot of time there, and some never escaped, or had the tools or will to do. Ragnar Persson has never been deceived by that particular demon; the work is consistently emotionally present, his art, like Tony Packo's Pickles, provide honest flavors.

All is folly, and with the descent of Michael Jackson, falling and falling and failing to find that most needed page-boy, not the faun-like doe-eyed boy he attempted to see in his mirrour, the one that flattered not, but the one that should have woken him each morning by shouting "Sir! Do not forget that you are a man!" or for Dash Snow, in the style of victorious Saladin, having an empty wood coffin presented as the perennial fore-runner of the *Vice Magazine* Do's and Don'ts. The streets of Stockholm's south side are truly far away, and the hipster youth flocking do not recognize the primary deities in their pop-culture cargo cult pageant. Now with death no longer the great equalizer, but instead where the hollow dried-up husk of existence gets transmogrified à la Calvin (and Hobbes!), replaced by the bright, shiny and eternally suave pop-meta iconic death of chink-free armor draping Ronnie James Dio, and a flawless façade where the dream-girls: pneumatic Pre-Raphaelite babeage, Megan Fox as Brunhilde, the cargo cult is aptly arriving as Bergman's Death will be hanging backstage with Iron Maiden's Eddie, regaling of Lady Di(e), and asking Charon if he can pay for the crossing of Styx with a vintage Mr. Roboto t-shirt. As they arrive on the other shore, they remove the double nickels from their eyes, finding themselves on the streets of Los Angeles or the Lower East Side or Stockholm, the perennial death-trip towns where the tyranny of the new is the tyranny of the old and the sun shone lacking alternative upon the eversame.

But death isn't Death, it is a mere fiction, and the plethora of visible death-trips in our popular culture have become the opposite of Holbein's *Dance Of Death*, they are more of a Protestant-derived counter-point to the popular Catholic death-bed How To manuals of the 17th and 18th century. In best case scenarios, like Ragnar's drawings, the symbolism becomes just like Opera Buffa, the grandest emotions, presented in the most spectacular ways, epic lead-motifs (heavy riffs) accompanying the fragile teenagers in the drawings, like Carmen being murdered to the sounds of the guitar-intro of "Reign in Blood." With the benefit of a portable dispenser of dreams, be it a ghetto-blaster, a cassette walkman or an Ipod, the remote actions in the most remote North become epic, thunderous, accompanied by sampled choirs from Orff's *Carmina Burana* set against the brutal and omnipresent guitar-chug-riffage.

Ragnar knows all this, and has probably felt it. There is evidence of such in one of his most masterful artists books, the disturbing yet triumphant *Teenage Lust* where it seems like he knows his Thomas Browne: that Life is a pure flame and we live by an invisible sun within us, even as the themes and the viewers eyeball-thrill is at its most stygian. Ragnar lifts the coins from our eyes repeatedly. He has shunned them from his own vision, like Nick Blinko, or Edward Burne Jones, or Simeon Salomon. Emotional landscapes overt, to counter-point inner landscapes that turn away from the world and its deceitful chatter.

I know Ragnar Persson's drawings as I once lived inside of them. A long time ago: In childhood, in adolescence. Like a song you heard a long time ago.

2009

13

Straight to Rare

Limited edition, numbered and signed, slipcased, on vellum, on large paper, gilded edges, all that has for a couple of centuries been fun and games courtesy of the rare book trade. Nowadays not such much anymore. Look around: Stuff is numbered, stuff is signed, stuff comes with a certificate of authenticity. Single malt whisky, art fanzines, psychedelic rock records on vinyl, gig posters, poetry booklets, replica reissues of historically significant:

Jeans
Wristwatches
Moccasin shoes
Documentary photography books
Proprietary pancake mix

In the age of hyper-fragmented cultural consumption, the stance is of immediate connoisseurship, as a fragmented overview of any topic can be assembled in the briefest sequence of google-klicks. But as this does not provide the sons and daughters of the bourgeoisie with the daily fiber requirement of a sense of importance and dose of one-upping self-worth, physical objects that indicate tradition and permanence as well as rarity and exclusivity need and must be purchased often and muchly. The act of choice has never been infused with more spiritual importance. The naming and identifying of the animist spirits provides the hunter and gatherer with the safe passage through the territory of the spirit. It can also provide the empowerment needed to capture it.

The identity and self-worth based on letting your pals know about what you know and what they don't know is now a matter of life, death and sustenance, especially if your chosen career is a pseudo-job based on perceived notions of with-it-ness and hipness within a demographic that your employer would like to sell products and/or services to. This can certainly be nerve-wracking, especially as the lugubrious variables of irony and heritage get thrown into the equation: ironic consumption, whether it is choices of tattoos, t-shirts, opening tracks on mixed tapes or ice cream toppings is the unpredictable variable that is used by the consumer to differentiate the self from the next guy/gal in competition for a job, a contract, a sex partner.

When played well, irony can provide moments of cultural epiphany that will have the person in question evermore identified as a non-linear cultural thinker, which in turn can result in promotions and raised salaries, all based on their choice of getting a tattoo of Charlie Sheen as Batman's Twoface, buggering a Sylvio Berlusconi dressed as Frank N. Furter. Or in musical terms, launching a literary career based on a mis-read of William S. Burroughs as Edgar Rice Burroughs and vice versa, or being the resident expert on Eastern European mid-70's jazz rock. The back of the medal (or the other side of Twoface's two faces) is the immense desire for products that somehow feel authentic, reek of authenticity or via osmosis make the consumer more authentic. This doubtlessly constitutes a simple inversion of ironic choice, and strangely enough corresponds well with it. The exclusive use of a (rare) North Maine beeswax hair pomade and arguing thread-count in (rare) madras shirts made in northern versus southern Chennai (up until mainstream new sincerity clowns Vampire Weekend name-checked madras upon which said topic was unceremoniously dropped) does not function in the same manner as code used to in pre-internet times. It isn't inclusive, it isn't a secret handshake where the purpose is to let the like-minded in, what it has instead become is a pure and unfiltered status signifier, like an uptown woman not only clutching her rare Birkin bag, but also holding a little banner that tells the world that the nuance of the leather of her handbag was exclusively available at a Hermès-sponsored bowling game betwixt Gwynny Paltyrow and Karla Bruny. The flaunting of the knowledge is solely about status, and the absolutely necessary self-deceit involved has to found itself on notions of quality, craftsmanship, egalitarianism, perpetuity, timelessness as *those are the sensibilities the consumer is trying to invoke*. It is all magical thinking, all self-congratulatory, all bullshit. It also feels like activism, like doing something, like making a stand.

And this is important as the bourgeoisie spend an inordinate amount of time in front of the screen, and said screen-time necessarily needs to feel important and meaningful, which means that basic time-wasters like blogging, shopping and chatting have to be infused with a sense of importance and social meaning. The serious possibility that most people don't care, and that the only ones who bother blogging, posting comments and voting up authentic restaurants and brands are the ones whose lives do not provide a corresponding empowerment and importance, can be chased away by the knowledge that those folks are more along the lines of people who weigh 400 pounds and fart pure unfiltered Chef-Boy-Ardee creating idealized hunky on-line avatars based on characters in video games. The notion that choices in cultural consumption elevates your social standing has chugged along most splendidly ever since the bourgeois hijacked all consumerist notions contained within quality, permanence, tradition and nobility from the upper classes and their rootin' tootin' rituals of courtly love. After having replugged the filling with theories of the picturesque and the commonality of the wilderness as God's grace, this meant that the only people ain't invited to the party are the great unwashed. Where ironic consumption and the new sincerity repeatedly meet is in the comments section on popular websites.

Check it out: people who aren't spewing racist/sexist/shmuckist garbage (as the screen and keyboard bring out the raging troll that always lived inside them) are posting comments with detailed connoisseuresque commentary on the subject matter at hand. An opinion will always be at the ready, and the opinion will always be flavored by one-upmanship and the flaunting of knowledge. It seems that the on-screen persona immediately becomes a public self as soon as the person interjects opinion. The desire to win, to aggressively one up, and to engage in some kind of dick-metaphor swordsplay.

Hey: not original think, but this should be pointed out once in a while: your screen avatar or-who are we kidding here-your Jungian shadow-self has become a societal safety-vent where steam is being let off and where things are being stated or indicated or strutted that would never be presented to a boss, a friend, a colleague or a spouse. Exclusive ownership of something that only you own and that most people can not identify as exclusive is an event-horizon of luxury consumption.

The guys and gals of new sincerity stifle a laugh as a school of Russians chug down Rodeo Drive padded by cardboard bags from Gucci and Prada. The 400 dollar lumberjack shirt, hand-stitched Michigan work-boots and rugged beard flaunted by the mid-management interactive tele-communications-types in big cities are an extension of this chuckle, no doubt. And the luxury brands are in on it, don't you know. Lumberjack shirts: Prada makes 'em. Artisanal Japanese ring-spun denim you can get at Dior. But that stuff is for the vulgarians. Your 400 dollar lumberjack shirt is authentic, and theirs ain't. So Anima meets Animus, they go on a date to a speakeasy decorated with taxidermy, serving 18-dollar Old Fashioneds spiced with house-made bitters and chilled with artisan ice. And here's the corker: they DON'T tell their friends about their night at the speakeasy, they only hint at it, as the new sincerity connoisseur-culture has reached a pure one-two punch of occult knowledge and magical thinking.

Occult knowledge solely empowers as long as it remains opaque or out of sight, and only is hinted at. Magical thinking means that the power of the totem-object will transfer to you. It means that your on-line comment about the only plausible place to eat a lobster roll in the eastern seaboard *will* lead to that promotion that you've been dreaming about, since your ability to project sincere and new connoisseurship knowledge in fields of clothing, food, culture-consumption and weekend-activities actualizes through said osmosis the kind of person you perceive yourself to be.

You aren't a consumer, bedazzled by the on-going ping-pong battle for your soul between Mammon and The Spectacle, you are a connoisseur, balancing hi- and lo-, knowing that the best drink to accompany the rare pleasure of a fried baloney sandwich is a rare vintage Dom Perignon.

2011

14

Genre Definitions, the Second-Guessing of Intent, and the Killed-By-Death-Style Punk Rock Rarity:

A Top Ten List in homage to Umberto Eco

As blogging, posting on boards, maintaining a web site or contributing regularly to professional music magazines really isn't suitable for my humors, please consider this column as what I provide instead of that. After having had my fragile little mind scrambled by Umberto Eco's recent book *The Vertigo of Lists* and its accompanying ultra-kickass exhibit at the Louvre, I decided to imitate in the fashion of a cap gun imitating a Sherman Tank. So here: I have a little list.

1.   More Glam, Pub and Pre-Punk Goodness

The particular amusement to my taste that is the hoarding of tone-deaf glam-stompers continues to resound under the scalp, has not lessened its glamorous grip. There's still no on-line discographies of note, even if hepcats like Robin Wills are letting plenty o' kittens out of the bag, so the only way to actually hear some of the dumbest songs in the history of rock is by the ol' trial and error method. You usually need to wade through 1000 singles for each promising-looking 45 that you purchase, and if your Utrecht-score numbers, say, fifty 7-inchers (which means that the tips of your fingers brushed against 50 000-odd 45's) wrapped in picture sleeves profoundly moronic in that continental glam kind of way, one out of ten of those will have sounds that provide the collars with the cuffs that match, which means that you'll walk home with five separate insights of pure thunka-drum flatulent-fuzztone gnosis. Those IQ 32 glam-stompers scratch an itch that otherwise can't be scratched, so therefore I will be seeing you at Utrecht year after year. The unk in the glam-junk, which ultimately is pre-punk, is certainly partially due to these records not being bally-hooed all over the place. I think that the appeal can be summarized as follows:

> **1:2** That the records are cheap. Don't forget that Killed by Death-style 70's punk was cheap up until the early 1990's, as were 60's punk records up until the early 80's.

> **1:3** That the reissues and repackaging and blogging has only just begun.

1:4 The thrill of being the first out of the blocks for the chase.

1:5 That the secret handshake is present in both marinade and meat: 45 distribution in Europe in the early seventies had proven itself worthy as a money maker for record companies big and small: people bought singles, you had a shot at getting on the charts every single week as there were a plethora of countdown radio shows, and some bands that grunted out two chord crud in 1972 had *huge* hits in the same way as other crude and cruddy bands had 6-7 years previously.

However: Some of the non-believers in the back are muttering that the reason that these obscure records are obscure is that they ain't good, and that when a lifelong consummate record collector starts binging on marginal niche genres it is usually evidence of a jaded palate. What are you gonna do. The years immediately prior to punk are very toothsome indeed for record collecting on the marginal tip. Not only are there not many reissues going around, there also are really very few writers reinterpreting records from 1970 – 1976 with punk back-way glasses on. This is good, as the records remain cheap, but this is bad, as one doesn't know what one is looking for until one finds it, which come to think is a thought both romantic and stoic. Marginal pub rock is where it is at. I remember back in the early 1990's, when I fraternized with the brilliant Victorian punk band Stiffs, Inc., and how members of said band could discuss the merits of the Stukas, the Lurkers, Wilko Johnson's Solid Senders and punk-era Downliners Sect in great detail, and with great passion. The *ouvre* of these *artistes* is inexpensive in its vinyl incarnation, and as my curiously raised eyebrows dance along to the 45 version of "Roxette," à la the Cadbury commercial, I can't but note how a lot of post-KBD collectors are instead choosing to spend their time weighing the merits of marginal power pop bands. I am certainly baffled by power-pop (as was I even way back in the when of the Greg Shaw *Bomp*-feature days), as I for the life of me couldn't hear anything but watered down commodifications of the raging blaze of the years prior. As I mentioned to an esteemed colleague the other day, as he was slogging through drafts on his introduction to a book collecting more of Shaw's *Bomp*-era waffles n' falafels, the LA & NYC & London-scenesters and biz-types who embraced power pop in 78/79/80 truly thought that they were on to the nextest biggest thing, and that the musical glory years of 65/66 were about to rise like a Phoenix and flush the great white toilet of pop culture hope from any noxious disco/hard rock build-up that the seventies had festered in their Platonic world of skinny-tie ideas. I think it was the other way around: marginal disco 12-inchers sound fantastic, and there are plenty of amazing major label hard rock albums to be had for cheap. Krautrock/ tranced-out psychedelic space rock fans might want to swallow the bitterest pills of their limited edition vinyl reissues and check out some Hawkwind/Hawklords/Status Quo if they haven't. And in the same breath, listening to power pop records marginal or mainstream just sounds like LA-cocaine-session-hack soft rock with narrower pants and lapels and worserer haircuts.Geoffrey Weiss, who often knows right from wrong, is rolling his eyes by now, as our 25-plus year friendship has taught him that I cannot be counted on to show any interest at all in melody, or for that matter, musicianship, or moreso the artistic craft of song-writing as a craftastic art, which probably means that I am disqualified from vexing and venting about, oh, power pop or soft rock or soft psych or orchestral pop or other sucky sucks. Well: I do want attitude, attitude, swagger, and attitude (good name for a law firm) from my rock & roll records, and as I know it, there is more of that to be found on Keggs records than Hollies records, or Electric Eels records rather than Plimsouls records.

2.   Ten Uncomped Unknown Uncharted Crazy 45's

The brutish tribalism that prevents the punk fan from embracing the rose petal-like art experiences contained within the voice of, say, Annie Lennox is the ADD hyper-focus that brings about a website devoted to the story of the Tapeworm 45, so dig we must where we stand.

Rare Killed by Death-style punk would seem to be an odd thing to go looking for at the Utrecht record fair, especially for someone as old to the game as yours truly. I will readily admit though that there is a fully internalized one-upmanship in finding uncharted, uncomped and unknown punk records from the seventies at this point in time. There are also records that are so rare that they aren't even really worth anything as far as monetary replenishment goes. They are too rare. The blogs haven't blogged about them, the dealers haven't noted them, the fanzines haven't ejaculated over them, they are too rare! Here are ten obscure KBD/DIY-type records. Some of 'em are truly too rare, some slept on, some only napped upon, maybe one or two is only medium rare and one might be well-done, I wouldn't know as I choose not to indulge in the round-the-ankle circle-jerk of on-line nekkid rekkid chat sites.

2:1   Dangerous Rhythm – Stray Cat Blues
(Orfeon Records, Mexico 1979)

For sheer otherness, this one's up there. Think I'll recycle Ryan Richardson's poignant statement about KBD-mannerisms yet again: for a record to truly bring that *KBD-feeling* to the party, it needs to be infused with an uncanny outsiderdom as executed by absurd men. Tapeworm is a perfect example of one, as is Chain Gang's "Son of Sam." This Mexican 1979 obscurity lands with a plop right between those two in the most exalted, most hallowed Valhalla of Amateurism. Deserves to be on every want list. The pubertal mud-howl of the vox, the speedfreak strum-chug of the unpunky hyper-Wilko guitar, and a rhythm section that must have made sense to the members of the band, and maybe to the members of the (French) Dogs before they learned how to play, but to the rest of us not such much. As otherworldly as I can imagine Hasil Adkins "She Said" must have seemed to the first rockabilly collector that unearthed one in those days of yore before the stale halitosis of historical proprietorship had consumed all the enthusiasm of that collecting sub-genre, negative-space style.

2:2　Subway Suck – I Sold My Ass For Rock & Roll
###　　　(Snowball Records, Norway 1977)

For the people familiar with the B-minus hard rock-y Subway
Suck album, the mythical beast that is this 1977-hyper rarity
must be resounding with plenty hype and less beefy umami.
Well: umami is in plentiful supply, and for those that consider
"Dog Eat Dog" by AC/DC a pre-punk anthem, this single is truly
the unheard masterpiece of Scandinavian 70's punk. The story
of how this was withdrawn prior to release, and how a singular
25-count left the (no doubt) splendid office of Snowball Records
32 years ago is well documented on many of the interwebs, but
nevertheless makes for a fascinating read. How threatening
and appalling the aesthetic language of punk was to your
regular everyday Sven and Inga 30-some years ago is oddly
congenial considering how a certain punky/gothy/emo-ey
Bambi-stance has reached an omnipotent rite-of-passage
actuality for Scandahoovian teenagers these days.

2:3　The Terrorists – Crazy Life 7"
###　　　(Rorschach Records, USA 1982)

I think it sounds early eighties, and the record certainly looks
like a West Coast record, so, hurray! Another mega-rarity! This
superb, noisy drum-machine-driven noisy fuzz-punk track came
to me via my London-based friend Jim, who has a voluminous
track record of unearthing insane records, and being the first to
do such. Luckily for me, late-70's/early-80's fuzz/noise slop isn't
his primi piatti, so he kindly let me bring this record back with
me. Repeated googling has resulted in oh sweet nuthin', asking
the inner circles of the rare punk Taliban what on earth is up
has resulted in Sweet FA, and repeated enjoyment of the disc in
question has had the jaw repeatedly drop to a point where one
is starting to resemble a Big Daddy Roth drawing. The a-side
has the same energy as those Endtables records, a Pere Ubu-ian
falling-forward stumbling propulsion that beggars repeat listen.
The flip is first-rate art-skronk DIY: like an inept MX 80 Sound.

2:4   Flying Calvittos – Lucky To Be Australian
(Groove Records, Australia 1980)

A strange noise-rock monstrosity from the nation behind, come to think of it, some of the finest records in the genre (SPK's "No More," Slugfuckers' "Deaf Disco," any early Tactics). This record however is hopelessly obscure, and doesn't have much of a reputation outside of the want lists of Oz-punk completists. That is wrong, wrong! The EP ranges from sick, amazing Electric Eels/X Blank X noise/art/punk howl to Residents-y blubber to the oddly anthemic klutzy and scrappy atmosphere of the title track. It is odd that this band sank without much of a trace, especially as it seems like they hailed from Sydney.

2:5   Rebel D'Punk – Mi Nueva Nacion
(Discos Cobra, Mexico 1984(?))

They are gods, what can I say? Now that the punk generation are counting their blessings and plucking their chickens and releasing documentaries and books left and right, quite often sounding like the four fellows in that Monty Python skit, attempting to trump each other in tales of suffering and hardship, at the same time as it is declared with a loud, calm, steady and geriatric voice that all the *real* punk had already died itself dead by, oh, March of 1975 or 6 or 7, it is as refresco as a piece of fresh mango with some chili, lime and salt to hear the rugged tough-guys of Rebel D'Punk blast one of the mightiest punk records I've ever heard, executed in the determinately un-punk/un-KBD year of 1984. They are gods, they are masters of the craft: The Cochran cover on the flip (loosely and I do mean as a goosely loosely) based on the Sex Pistols version, is in stark competition Mexican-wrestler-style for the championship belt today and anyday. These men are kings of punk, gods of punk.

2:6   The Dogs – Cette Ville Est Un Enfer
      (Philips Records, France 1980)

2:7   The Fuzz – Satan's Fans
      (Cime Records, France 1981)

2:8   Gerard Depardieu – La P'tite Agathe
      (Philips Records, France 1980)

I love the French. I love their wine, their food, the landscapes, even the Parisians, and I do really love their punk. I always thought that French punk was an unfair recipient of collector scum slappage, and as I just navigated through a stack of big-name big-legend big-price American punk monsters, and didn't find enough musical merit to let them remain in their respective grease-puddle on the record shelf (Decadents, Jackie Shark, Absentees), I'd like to contrast and compare with a troika of French records that I think are much unfairly slept on, and hence quite inexpensive, notwithstanding their substantial rarity. "Satan's Fans" by Fuzz was one of those records that I kept asking everyone about for years. Have you heard it? Have you seen it? Do you know anyone with a copy?

The usual (wonderful) ordeal. As Stuart Schreder pointed out on his exemplary website shitfi.com, the presence of a record on the want lists of (so called) big name fans will always result in it being added to the want list of the lesser-big name fans, and the Gordian knot will roll down the hill and snowball before Sisyphus puts his copy up for sale on Ebay.* One remains baffled by The Dogs instinctive understanding of many rock idioms. On this one, Sterling Morrison would have been mighty pleased to hear "Eight Miles High" played in a Velvets-setting,

* The logical end-game being that the drummer decides to google his former band one day, then to his amazement finds out how much his old record is worth and starts selling off the 490 copies he has left of the 500 copy pressing.

115

and on the flip a perfect example of The Dogs stanza circa "Walking Shadows" (ultimately I think their best album), a voice as singular as anybody working in that odd and strict 70's/80's record collector rock flavor; Flamin' Groovies, Nuggets, Dave Edmunds, MC5's *Back In The USA*, you know the drill. I think this was issued as a bonus 7" with that exceptional album. Ultimately, I think the Dogs will be worshipped as masters of the craft in the same manner as the heroes of the Dogs late lead singer/lead record collector Dominique. Right about now seems to be a time as good as any to listen to Gerard Depardieu's best punk howl as exemplified on a promo-only 45 where Bijou (remember them?) are backing Gerard on "La P'tite Agathe," a mere lunch-munch 60 second speed punk blast, issued as the flip of Jane Birkin moaning through a Bible segment set to crap reggae—a soundtrack to a Serge Gainsbourg flick called *Je Vous Aime*. I know you don't think so, but this record exists and is pretty damn good!

2:9   Cyklon Og Anti-Cyklon
(No label, Denmark 1981)

This Danish 1981-noise/mess must be celebrated as possibly the finest slice of flatulent scrape-noise-punk-freeform I've heard. An astonishing racket: noisy psych-punk à la Fuckin' Flyin A-Heads mingled with fantastic Fall-esque noise-throb. My oh my. Those speakers be blistering. This Sort Sol-related mess was considered one of those impossible records for years (50 copies pressed, hand-cut sleeves made from old maps, rubber-stamped labels, you've heard the story before) but this has recently shown up as a more-or-less facsimile reissue, difficult to discern from the (no doubt) much more toothsome original!

2:10 Vega Menighet – EP
(Flass Records, Norway 1981)

In 1981, the anything-goes trickle of independent record production had reached the 15-year old Dag Marius who recorded and released this EP with his pal Oddbjorn Edvardsen. The record is monstrously amazing: God-Walks-Among-Us doofus/inept/in-joke DIY nonsense, lacking even in the most base notions of communicating with anyone except the voices inside their heads and the autistic-identical-twin dialogue that (I gather) prevailed throughout the recording process. The UK artists Sue Webster and Tim Noble built a sculpture a few years ago that I've always dug: it is called "Two Dirty Fucking Rats" and consists of a pile of kitchen garbage, fast food containers and general rubbish that, as it has a light source projected upon it, casts a shadow that looks exactly like a couple of rats having sex. Well: the Vega Menighet EP, as it spins on the gramophone, casts a large shadow, but one of abject beauty where this ballistic teenage in-joke provides some sort of gnosis on the brilliance of unfettered creativity and its resulting monument to the absurd man.

>>>SPECIAL BONUS TRACK<<<

2:11 Geitost – Imorra Babylon (Bröd Records, Norway 1981)

The a-side consists of an anti-cop noise frenzy (I think this must've been some kind of street theatre protest project) that funnels straight into howled-vox boogie-rock/DIY with one of the most plinka-plunka guitar solos I've ever heard plunka-plinka'd. The whole mess is wildly out of tune, and more on the psychotic side than the band name which translates as "goat cheese" would imply. The b-side is super-fried hippie/noise DIY, sort of like Here & Now, but crazy, completely crazy! Not that we are going to start trusting Wikipedia at this point, but according to them/it/satan the main guy in the band, the poet and green activist Jan Bojer Vindheim, is sorta embarrassed of his guitar solo and doesn't like to fess up to his involvement. Write him a fan letter! I am sure he has a few hundred copies left to sell you.

3.   Ten KBD-style monster tracks that are way cheap

And here are ten that are super-easy to find that most definitely deliver the same bang for far less buck than all those Butchy Butch and the Butch Butchers.

3:1   Rost – Levande Rost 7" (R&P Records, Sweden 1981)

A perfect example of a band that would most likely have gotten pissed off if they'd been accused of being punky, but nevertheless: This hyper-charged and blitzkrieged take on Willie Dixon's "I Just Want To Make Love To You" sounds positively Stoogian. The ripping leads are in the James Williamson pocket, and the disintegrating rhythm section could be a pair of intoxicated Asheton brothers. The intent was certainly not punk; what we have here is a certain kind of rarified Stockholm-record-collector-rock. The sounds streaming out of my speakers, tho', are as punked out as all get.

3:2   Swell Maps – Dresden Style (Rough Trade, UK 1978)

Thousand-dollar-stare water-closet fuzztone slop from a band that never stepped sideways and never delivered inferior product even if they at times intently attempted such. The barn-peeling and paint-storming guitar solo on "Dresden Style" is Oscar the Grouch inviting Tommy Gunn from the Pagans to record inside his trash can. This record has been erroneously priced at 5-15 dollars on Interbay, where the correct tag should have been in the lower four figures, as we all know that musical merit is what steers the hand clutching the Paypal wallet.

3:3 Devo – Penetration in the Centerfold (Virgin, UK 1979)

John Spencer, whose taste has always been better than his music, covered this insane art/punk audio-self-destruct with his first band Pussy Galore (it is probably the best thing they ever did). I love Devo, and have over the years been enough of a wally to acquire CDRs of early demos, live concerts, outtakes and all that. The early years in Akron, Ohio circa 1973-1976 are twined with the American pre-punk hep, and the rabid attack of this record hints at this frenzied sludge having its origin early on in the band's career, but that's just a guess. As this is the flipside of "The Day My Baby Caught Me Surprise," which was a big record, one of the few American art-punk 45s that can rival SPK's "No More" or Mittageisen's "Hardcore" can be had for mere cereal money.

3:4 Jilted John – Jilted John (Rabid Records, UK 1978)

I think that the pinnacle of record production that was ever reached by Joy Division producer Martin Hannett was certainly not the two albums they did together, nope. You got to say nope when you can't say yep. Martin Hannett in my book was more the wally responsible for taking the awesome Stooges/Pagans/Motorhead live-blaze of Joy Division and turning it slightly fruity. Fully knowing that legions of doomed dorm dorks have digested these two albums with a gusto that they possibly should have reserved for Philadelphia cheese steak sandwiches, I do think that the merits of this great rock band do not correctly correspond with their studio output. Hannett can be directly blamed for the water-closet ker-splash of the gated snare drum and the festering coagulations of digital reverb that f---ed the collective s--- up in eighties and nineties "alternative" record production. This was exemplified on the baroquely grotesque *Unknown Pleasures* and *Closer* LPs: not in a way necessarily unpalatable, but as those LPs became a norm for how to execute quality audio in a recording studio, sort of like

Making Movies or *Brothers In Arms* for people dressed in black with short hair, the imitations mostly ended up as sucko. Well: as his production on the Jilted John single is certainly the pinnacle of a career that later on came to include records that either don't sound so good or sound too good (depending on what side of the tracks one is keeping ones nose on), one should acknowledge this amazing single, as one acknowledges his other production masterpieces like *Spiral Scratch* and the *Times Up* bootleg. Or maybe they are two different people? Martin Hannett likes digital delay and Martin Zero likes snacky and crunchy punk guitars. Jilted John was not only *the* punk-cash-in novelty hit of 1978, leading to a myriad of superb TOTP-appearances (google! youtube!) and half-assed novelty follow-ups, but more so a stunning punk record complete with A Guitar Sound worthy of comparison to the Honey Bane single on Crass Records or the Opus' "The Atrocity" 45. The base festering attack of this mighty tune is fueled by the kind of demented teenage audacity that seems to reach the mainstream chart nevermore, sadly enough.

3:5   Lurkers – Shadow (Beggars Banquet, UK 1977)
3:6   Lurkers – Ain't Got A Clue (Beggars Banquet, UK 1978)

At some point in the yore of my *Ugly Things*-hacking, I dismissed these gents as lager-crappy Lurkers, attempting shallowly and stupidly to prove some long-forgotten point about a pricey KBD-record I thought should be less pricey. Well: The lager-crappiness of the Lurkers is exactly the reason that these records are the sun-rise exercise of choice for any 70's punk record-raker that has figured out that the records that spill most often on the turntable ain't necessarily the pricey ones. I hereby place the Lurkers' humble hair pie in my face as we need lager-crappy punk in our lives like the fish needs chocolate. These two 45s, both substantially cheaper than a pint of lager, are intoxicating sturm-und-drang that seems to sound better by the decade. Ridiculing the Lurkers in favor of, oh I dunno, the Horrible Nurds or "I Gave My Punk Jacket To Richie" is the kind of conduct that signifies the need for a spectator while we blast records on the ol' gramophone. Is this the kind of nonsense that music blogs are leading us towards? Mea maxima culpa!

3:7   The Rings – I Wanna Be Free (Chiswick, UK 1977)

Epically shmucky thug-trad-by-numbers rocker-punk blaze executed by aging hippies not willing to let the green-haired young-uns spin dough-nuts around them as they were bombarded with alpaca skid-marks.** Both sides of this chirpy cheapie (you'll have money left for the chippy) proves that thug-punk was the mastered domain of the (ex) hippie.

3:8   The Kursaals – Television Generation (CBS, UK 1977)

There's evidence that every member of the Kursaal Flyers were sporting humungous Jeff "Skunk" Baxter-style moustaches, Great Gatsby-baggies and those knitted multi-colored pull-overs during the very recording of this single, and that the short-haired skinny-tie-dudes flamboyantly punk-draped in an alleyway on the picture sleeve were the nephews of the band. Muff Winwood producing, and a Feelgoods/Kilburns 12-bar chug b-side tells the tale of aging pub rockers punking out to pay the rent. Not that there's anything wrong with that. You can certainly hear that Winwood brought some sort of punk awareness with him to his work on the first Dire Straits*** album a couple of months after this session. This record is one of the finest examples of expert musicians dumbing it down for the proverbial kids, a tactic that has failed every single time its been attempted since the advent of time.

** Alpacas are master spitters. – Edumucational Ed.

*** I can't even begin to say how good it feels to know that Dire Straits will be found in a google search of my name! Not once but twice in one article! As I might be picking a bit of a dust-up as I type, dare I mention that the similarities in sound betwixt Dire Straits and Television should be stage-whispered during those rules and protocol meetings that'll be structured once the mid-managers of the punk-apocalypse will start getting it together to make a move-on.

3:9   Blurt – Get (Test Pressings, UK 1981)

Collecting KBD-style punk is usually not alright (or compatible) with liking saxophones. An exception here tho': the b-side of the effortlessly pastoral, wide-open and screechingly noisy classic "My Mother Was A Friend Of An Enemy Of The People" is an insane barnacle of scuzzy-punk energy that could find its way to its inclusion as a potent pizza-topping at a collector scum one-upmanship afterparty.

3:10   Tears – Tonight (Sonet, Sweden 1978)

Can't seem to get enough of that grill-punk sound: you know the kind, slightly too constipated, too swishy "the lady doth protest too much, methinks" tough-guy antics, a hard-rock/ NWOBHM-flavoring agent, and a general smegmoid bar-band atmosphere that at some point must have resulted in the disc being returned to the dollar bin with a sneering yeech from the KBD-aficionado. Well: these records are sounding better and better aren't they? The flaming discovery and glutted prices of Hurriganes records, and the increased attention placed to metalloid punk of the late 70's/early 80's, proofreads the pudding. Tears were a glam rock band that released three LP's of varying snackability (the second is the best one, and contains a couple of tasty glam-slop slices), and by 1978 were delighted to be included in the Sonet Records series of sleeveless red vinyl seven-inchers devoted to *the new thing*. The series might be notable for a couple of pretty good records (Heartbreak Hotel, Hangover) and some more aligned to the totalitarian A&R sketchiness of a 1978 medium-sized record company wanting a bit of that new short-haired rock & roll without offending the long-haired executive management.

4. The Penguin Café Orchestra

"I am the proprietor of the Penguin Café, I will tell you things at random."

"Random" is how my children refer to amazing things out of the ordinary. When Simon Jeffes woke from a fever dream, this is what he took with him from his personal sanctified Other Place. He decided to form a band with the aim of performing music of human visceral immediacy and simplicity. He succeeded, hopefully beyond his wildest expectations.

"What I heard was straight from the source, why it is we play music, that gut level sound of humans being human. There was a joy to it, an ease and integrity straight from the stomach and the heart. It wasn't mediated by the mind at all."

White soul, like the Feelies, like watching an old ska record collector step out of his jadedness and commence that two-footed shuffle when the drive of the tune can't help him from starting to shimmy like his sister Kate is ultimately a holy moment: the strife of love in a dream. In the summer of '77, Jeffes orchestrated music honoring the queen of England's silver jubilee, at the same time as he was getting paid by Malcolm McLaren and the Sex Pistols for work he was doing for them. Somewhere within that exceptional ability in playing double nickels on the dime is the core iconoclastic splendor of the Penguin Café Orchestra. Jeffes favorite comment about PCO was made by a Japanese girl at a concert: "This music is strange," she said, "it sounds like music I heard a long time ago."

5.   Lars Hollmer and Von Zamla

The track "Harujänta" reverberates in my expatriate soul with the power of a childhood summer food. His recent death had me reach for his records, and what he did within a Scando-folk plus RIO-idiom is nothing short of amazing.

6.   Thinking Fellers Union Local 282

The effortless brilliance of Thinking Fellers Union Local 282 makes me wonder how long it'll take for this lengthy slew of albums to be rediscovered by you young people. 40-somethings and 50-somethings end up distributing a lot of gum-flap spittle in regards to the times and bands and shows and drugs and sandwiches they were *there* for, so I'll just take my faux-finished ass over and get in line: When I consider the bands that I was involved with in capacities of varying dubiance during my youth-man years, I can only really think of Union Carbide Productions, Os Mutantes, Thomas Jefferson Slave Apartments, The Monks, Chain Gang and Slayer to round out a list with Thinking Fellers Union Local 282 on it. In the late eighties and early nineties, they by far superceded their indie-rock cred brethren and sisthren:

6:1 The propulsion and attack and sheer crunchy noise (especially live) out-stripped all those bands with autopsy album covers and lyrics about baby-eating that festered in the Midwest and on the Lower East Side.

6:2 For absurd tunings and abject tonalities that never ceased to dazzle, surprise and amuse—all done with a sense of wonder and/or discovery devoid of big-city east coast insider smirk— they were positively Circle X-esque and Circle X-ian.

6:3 And when it came to pure psychedelic mind-melt fuckery, they were the only band that I saw that came close to Butthole Surfers flawless disarray, when the Butthole Surfers were at their prime circa 1986-1988.

TFUL282 remained marginal, underground and utterly beloved by their small legion of fans. I think it all seemed too goofy, and their dismissive attitude to image and (constipated tough-guy) stance has prevented them from reaching the post-cause legend of all those sucky bands from the same era. TFUL282 were superbly insulated and self-indulgent, each one of their albums devoted in equal proportions to carefully administrated and orchestrated sound-craft and rehearsal space boom-box slop. Their origin in Iowa and transplant to that capitol of self-aware outsider braggadocio, San Francisco, all but make perfect sense as one considers their brilliant heritage with extended and elastic 20/20-backwards specs. I always thought of TFUL282 when one of my (older) record collecting buddies attempted to get me pumped up over San Francisco sixties psychedelia. TFUL282 were truly the kind of musical mind melt that I expected but didn't get out of those Quicksilver Messenger Service and Jefferson Airplane records, lo-fi as they were, the multi-directional super-dynamic barrage of the first four albums makes them absolute classics of their era. What TFUL282would have sounded like all along with "proper" record production is one of those armchair quarterback shoulda-coulda-wouldas that rock fandom reverberates with. As I listen to the meticulous sound craft of Bob Weston's production (always superior in skill to his odious boss Steve Albini) on the later records, I can't but think a little thunk of what he would have done to the mighty but (intentionally) lo-fi early albums.

7.   **Lux Interior: RIP**

Lux Fiat!

The storyline in Arthur Machen's short story "The Inmost Light" where the soul of a scientist's wife is trapped within a jewel by him, but where this process brings an all-consuming otherness to the remainder of her day, is an apt metaphor for how the music of the Cramps enters ones psyche, certainly steals your soul, but happily leaves it residing within your body together with a lifelong illumination, an illumination that stays within. Your internal light will guide you. That life ends for other people isn't surprising or shocking, even as the notion of our own death is impossible and intellectually absurd, which in some cases brings us snuggly into the lap of religion, where the alternative lonely singing-in-the-rain-style tap in an un-wanting void devoid of meaning feels emotionally unpalatable, in turn bringing us on controlled quests for oblivion. As our neon meat dream of an octafish continues, we stumble on towards darkness and the towering silhouette of time in conquest. A rapidly diminishing future cannot be vexed with an accumulated past of qualitative reality, as counter-point to the quantitative reality that remains for us.

As Lux Interior breathed for 62 years, this breath infused us all with meaning. The records land repeatedly on the gramophone, and the people who exclusively prefer their early work are not paying attention to the stoic reality of how the passing of time works. The turmoil that his death set off inside me had me reach for all their albums, and I can say that the power of the work never receded much or at all. Check out "Let's Get Fucked Up" from 1996's *Flamejob*. The last time I saw the Cramps was the best gig I saw them do, that after having attended a myriad gigs executed by a cornucopia of lineups.

Such joy a mere mortal has in the presence of divinity, such elevation as when earth, water, fire and air, came together in this garden fair, wrapped in leopard skin, snake skin and vinyl, motorized with the breath of the ancient and justified.

Lux Interior (gnosis) as Lux E Tenebris: light out of darkness.

8.   The Feelies 1977 demo tape

As bright as the whitest Velvets, and almost as hot.

9.   Tesco Vee invented Killed By Death

I was just glancing at the Magna Carta of 70's punk collecting, and it sure ain't *KBD #1*. It is an article Tesco Vee wrote for the July 1984 issue of *Maximum Rock & Roll*. The wonderment and enthusiasm of uncharted territory formally gleams like a golden shower of non-hits, splashing over the fade-to-gray MRR newsprint: Alas, the map was on the territory. The front-man of a classic first generation 'zine (*Touch & Go*) *and* the buyer at a classic record shop (Dearborn, Michigan's Schoolkids) *and* the vocalist for a punk/hardcore-overlap/over-slop band of great merit (the Meatmen) is furthermore a friggin' oracle when it comes to the ins n' outs of the 70's punk collecting maze.

I feel morally obliged to quote at length from this article. Dude:

OK, so what if we were in the wrong place at the right time... so what if we would have given our collective left nuts to see some of those legends... the fact remains we could console ourselves with the little slabs of plastic that we somehow fondled like they were glasses of Ghandi's urine... these discs were somehow special... we know not why... we documented our love for these precious mammy's in our own rag... at they traversed the turntable they were written about/listened to/came upon/etc... the 7" piles grew larger at alarming rates... the feeling that you somehow had this hidden knowledge that nobody else had about this vibrant subculture...

The Classy Fred Blassie of punk. The front cover of this issue of MRR, illustrating Tesco's article, features pics of 45s like, oh, the Negative Trend EP, Rotters "Sink The Whales," Necros "Sex Drive," Fresh Color's eponymous, and the Huvudtvätt 7" to name a few. Onwards fellow pencil-neck geeks! Onward! This was 1984, and these records were not only hard to find already back then, but imagine searching for these discs without interwebs or ebays or popsikes. It seems, if one is to commence a web search or ten, daily, accompanied by the same search on Ebay (rare KBD is a good one), then one will surely notice how the audience for rare KBD has grown exponentially as new punters are added: the jams themselves become available for everyman, first as home-recorded mixed tapes, then as compilation LPs, then as CD reissues of the LPs, then as home-burned CDRs, then downloads, then streams. Our endgame zone with all our secret handshakes, keeping Punky Bambi away from the people that really truly were the ones who killed her has been eradicated as Hot Topic opens it 750th retail store. If these statements need to be followed by some hard science, I would suggest that a glance is made at the following equation, where "X" is the number of Ramones t-shirts sold before the band broke up, and "Y" is the perceived efficiency of the logo to boost the sense of self-worth of the mall-shopping adolescent. The same equation can be put into play where "X" are the number of copies of a rare KBD-style masterpiece that the group in question sold during the duration of their tenure, and the "Y" is the number of times that a "unique" opportunity to obtain this "mega-rarity" has occurred on Ebay.

The terminology certainly has changed: we need new words. Rare records, or hyper-rare records, or impossibly rare mega-rarities that only show up this once and is your only chance in this your only visit on this planet to obtain this particular mega-punk KBD-rarity, are phrases that we can no longer under any circumstances trust, as the record that is impossible to obtain *is* possible to obtain, as a copy has made itself available for sale right in front of you on the bleakly bluish pale of your computer screen. And then you go to Popsike and forget about it; *ten* copies of the same record have sold on Ebay in the past two years. If a once-in-a-lifetime hugga-mugga-mega-giga-rarity has shown up that often, then what are rare records? Are there rare records? Does it matter that the record is rare? A streamed version of the track is available on the Black Denim Mouth-breather Blog. Quite enjoyable too, (barely) reverberating through those tinny computer speakers. Lo-fi and all that. And you don't have to spend 800 bucks to own those sounds pressed onto plastic at some point in the past pastures of yore. How come it doesn't feel that great? Look at that event horizon: all those tracks, all that punk. Ones and zeros in row after row.

10. Disco Rules. As does early hip hop. And early techno. But only if it is primitive.

The splendid youth-combo the Dirtbombs are about to release an album of cover versions of early Detroit techno jams. The record is fantastic: bringing in a krautrocky droniness to the primitive sounds of electronic necessity that streamed out of Detroit in the early eighties, in themselves a masterful continuation of the early disco-rap sounds of the South Bronx and the delightfully inept private press disco 12"s pressed up throughout the USA in the wake of the mass-market success of disco in the late seventies. These are great sounds of primitive American music, no less amazing and rewarding than the (superior) American reconfiguration of British punk (KBD!), or the (superior) American reconfiguration of British invasion (60's Punk!). Open up your ears to some new flavors, handsome.

Start here:

> Cybotron – Cosmic Cars
> Rhythim is Rhythim – Strings Of Life
> Skip Jackson – Microwave Boogie
> Lonnie Love – Young Ladies
> A Number of Names – Sharevari
> Bob Chance – It's Broken
> Sessomatto – Sessomatto
> Nice & Nasty 3 – The Ultimate Rap
> T Ski Valley – Catch The Beat
> Model 500 – No UFOs

2010

15

Hitler is on YouTube

There are oodles of anonymous YouTube clips devoted to Hitler in the bunker at the tail-end of WW2. Hitler bitches about Wii. Hitler is pissed off that Paul Stanley from Kiss is a bad visual artist, he's upset that Kiss are touring without "Space-Ace and the Cat-Man," he throws tantrums about the Superbowl, all set to the same four minute excerpt from the critically super-acclaimed and serious masterpiece, the 2004 film *Downfall*.

There are problems with enjoying these clips: A veneer of banal comedy applied to the greatest horrors of the 20th century, the copyright-infringing juvenile guffawing at a substantial slice of cinematic art, Hitler becoming a cartoon character, and therefore seeming less evil to those who are as removed from World War 2 as my generation is removed from Victorian England. Well: hooey I say. Guffawing at evil men or depictions of evil men is a categorically good thing in my book. The potency of Adolf Hitler, taken *reductio ad absurdum* into an Eric Cartman with a problematic Vienna-era Ultravox haircut, and the emotional stability of a five year old injected with Cinnamon Toast Crunch extract via enema-syringe, brings about a most useful reaction in the people who are too removed from the events to respond with a knee-jerk. The moment in 1945 when the gates of hell were thrown wide open to the world and hell itself was presented as a man-made organizational war-bureaucracy formally executed to dispose of the bodies connected to the societal structures and pockets of wealth that the common nazi thieves needed to seize in order to fuel a machinery of war, which as any historian will point out is a necessity for the plunderer to keep his plundery going. Ask Attila. Ask one of the Khans. The Hitler clips help bring out a reissue of a knee jerk response. This helps us identify the totalitarian hob-goblinery of a petty dictator, who is shown as laughable and responsible for shitty behavior that simply isn't acceptable, à la *The Office* at its best or reality television at its worst.

When we kackle like your uncle Sal at "Hey Whazzup Make Up" by Passing Stones,[7] the sublime recontextualized Rolling Stones' video (by StS, the same genius that brought us the "Shreds" Youtube clips[8]) that in its endgame brings us the hyper-reality of a bunch of absurd middle-aged rock dinosaurs chump-changing us with a card-board-cut-out-cartoon-rebellion with even less fiber and nutrition than that Cinnamon Toast Crunch enema I mentioned earlier, we inch closer to a resolve of the problems brought by your sides aching of convulsive laughter upon repeated viewing of the Hitler clip where he finds out about Oasis canceling their tour. In "Passing Stones" Mick Jagger spouts a bunch of gibberish that resonates closer to a truth unspoken about the absurdity of rock & roll commerce, not unlike the games of anagram in Brandan Kearney and Gregg Turkington's milestone of corporate rock & roll culture détournement, their sublime book *Warm Voices Rearranged: Anagram Record Reviews*. Every movement by the Stones and their singer is mocked by our maestro STS, parodying the swollen rock licks and the flaunty rock vocal gestures with absurdities that resonate like the very best détourned comic books from the Situationist sixties.

The major record companies and film companies compulsively removing their copyrighted material from YouTube or adding trite commercials and advertising banners to their footage (on the occasion of them allowing it to be viewed) increases the viewer's alienation from the given mainstream swill exponentially. The people who consume culture with the fervor needed to seek it out on YouTube are increasingly disgusted by what they are served, like a cultural McDonald's slowly but steadily increasing the time period that the hamburger is allowed to rest under the heat lamp. This is what is reflected by the increase in the utilization of the imagery and musics of 60's thru' 80's mainstream rock/pop swill in montage, collage and détournement. The YouTube Shreds series are the perfect example. Reducing the sounds made by

---

7 http://www.stsanders.com/www/pages/videos/band-shreds/sts-rolling-stones.php
8 Archived at http://www.stsanders.com/www/pages/videos.php

now-geriatric rock dinosaurs of yore to a cartoonish soundtrack going alongside their cartoonish mannerisms and stanzas: "I Will Never Go To School" by Piss is set to "I Was Made For Loving You" by Kiss, and "Hey Whazzup Make Up" by Passing Stones is set to "Start Me Up" by the Rolling Stones.

This style of détournement actually works within a more serious realm than taking the mickey out of pathetic geriatric rockers; a quick way to find out just how nasty your local, national or global oppressor actually is is to present a détournement of the particular brand or flavor of poison they are guilty of spreading. "Billy Mays Can Help" or "Autotune the News" or any number of Sarah Palin edits and remixes reveal content and true nature in the same manner as Duchamp's greatest hits or Tex Avery's cat that hated people: what was only apparently real is brought into a vacuous hyper-reality where we ourselves must identify evil notwithstanding what level of cartoonization it is presented to us on, as newsmedia falters, and as school books get re-edited from a political slant and as a thought-police of the industrial revolution boogie to a brand new beat of dislodging of truth in information. Swiftian and Rabelaisian satire is alive and well and creating situations on the (goddamn) internet.

2011

16

60's Punk Compilations*

The commencement of the 60's Punk compilation in the wake of *Nuggets* and *Pebbles* is shrouded in secretive assembly, exercises in obscurist taste, subterranean connoisseur-ship, secret-handshake knowledge and one-upmanship up the yingyang. All those whispered secrets of the disenfranchised middle-class white-boy college-boy inner city-junkie-boy of the seventies, eighties and nineties have now come to pass as a ruling paradigm for how beyond-the-pale rock music consumption is directed in blog-dom, on-line mag-dom, bit-torrent stream-dom, and how the necessary strands of elitism are perpetuated in an era where ownership of a musical artifact not-so-much determines the egoboo as the knowledge of the artifact's existence. The tasty morsels of deep-fried metaphorical gristle on my plat du jour are 60's punk compilations. A recent field of fevered collecting, outpacing recent record collector micro-trends like minimal synth, junk shop glam and California singer-songwriter is the pursuit of the rarest vinyl comps of 60's punk that were issued in the early-mid 80's. These compilations are filled choc-a-bloc with some of the most thrilling sounds that are out there. But I don't have to tell that to the informed readership, as the informed readership:

> Bought the comps when they came out,
> In some cases, compiled them,
> Already know most everything that I write in this article,
> Disagree with everything I say,
> can command the direction of the traffic outside their window
> utilizing strange and ancient Jedi mind-control powers.

It is a bit of a natural after-the-end-of-the-world, or at least after-the-end-of-the-record-shop conceptual finality that what started as consumer guides that were prepped to spread the knowledge about some rare and tasty sounds (with a healthy spread of collector-scum one-upmanship on top) have turned into a premier-status desired commodity. Pressed in editions that in many cases were as small as

---

* The term "60's punk" is better than "garage" and was used back when.

135

the original 45s compiled, wrapped in hand-made-looking packages, and with liner-notes that read like a copy of *Black To Comm* had mated with a sports-blog, these artifacts are rightfully fetishized as capable of providing the white middle-class collector with a more than adequate block-stop for that aching void of his or us or mine. The dividing line between sercon and fannish is a natural in the history of the 60's punk compilation album: albums that are basically fannish, i/e jumbles of insane garage punk 45s in an attempted palatable and amusing order, are in counterpoint to the comps that are sercon: regional compilations, or compilations where a given producer or a given label will provide "historical" parameters for the music. It will come as no surprise that I vastly prefer the prior, and that notwithstanding the subtle beauty in challenging oblivion and/or our-lord-and-master in a crusade or quest to find out as much as is possible to know about a band or a label or the music in a small town in the Midwest back in the whenever, ultimately what erupts out of them there loudspeakers usually benefits the most from the sublime editorializing of the mind of an aesthete. Like the gents behind *Open Up Your Door* or *Scum Of The Earth* or *Back From The Grave*. The temptation to include crap cuts wrapped up neatly in a geographical or economical context can indeed be far too tempting, with the end-game result that Punky Bambi reaches for *High In The Mid Sixties volume 24* far less often than she reaches for *BFTG #5*, and that therefore when Punky Bambi decides to digitize some choice 60's punk cuts for her blog, the tracks from *BFTG #5* get heard more often and the ones from *HITMS #24* less so. Fannish beats sercon, hands down.

I started buying 60's Punk/garage compilations in the Fall of 1982. Friends of mine pointed out that you could purchase cut-out copies of *Nuggets* in its Sire Records incarnation, as well as cheap copies of *Pebbles* volume 9 and 10 from Ginza, the biggest of the Swedish cut-out mail order houses, where we furthermore bought cheapo copies of albums by the Seeds, the Sonics, the Chocolate Watch Band, and the Standells.

My friends, who were older than me, provided context for the albums (*so you think you are a punk kid, you know nothing*) and motivated us to form a band playing Count Five, Seeds and Kim Fowley covers. The first two volumes of *Back From The Grave* were purchased in 83/84, and were so much better than anything else on the market, that I remember the listening experience ended up feeling a bit baffling. To this day, as most collectors of the genre will attest, nothing else comes close, pretty much. And in that "pretty much" I compile this list of my favorite 60's punk/garage compilations with the *BFTGs* on top. The 60's punk compilation narrative also contains the fascinating story of independent record shops of the 1980's, especially those that put together mail order catalogues. In Sweden, it was Musik & Konst in Malmö, which was one of the few outlets in the old country for you to obtain 60's punk comps, alongside obscure US-import seven-inchers, fanzines and bootleg LP's by the Velvets and the Cramps. As I spent my teen years in the absolute boonies, these mail order catalogues were lifelines of hep, and they also provided aesthetic directives in a manner much more efficient (and important to us) than the Brit music weeklies, radio, or even fanzines. As we started to order from overseas mail order operations like New York's Midnight or London's Plastic Passion (we had already been buying from Small Wonder and Rough Trade for years, but RT weren't on the 60's punk/neo-garage thing, and I think Small Wonder had gone out of business by then), we were able to locate more obscure stuff, and in some instances original copies of the compiled records. When the illustrious Stefan Kery of Stockholm's mighty fine Stomachmouths combo (and the future honcho of the Subliminal Sounds label) became the buyer for the Vinyl Mania import record shop circa 1984/1985, garage-punking Scandahoovians found themselves in the enviable position of being able to purchase pretty much anything that they'd desire from the Hallowed Halls of Collector Scum Valhalla. I remember original Plan 9 Misfits singles for five bucks a pop, and the first Pussy Galore EP with a store-sticker announcing one OK garage-punker and three experimental clunkers. The fanaticism among 60's punk fans resulted in the development of a global road map: bands devoted to the 60's punk cause in Italy, in Spain, in France and in Midwestern American towns. There were fanzines, mail-order sources for the fanzines (Sweden had an amazing one in the catalogues of Gunnar Johansson), record shops, venues and bands, bands and more bands. The resounding us-versus-them of this scene collapsed quite rapidly like the house of cards it probably was: The scene rapidly fragmented into micro-scenes along the lines of the ones we see everywhere today. The bands that were into 1965 garage didn't get along with the ones who were into 1967 garage-psych; the bands who mixed the garage sound with other punk strands didn't get along with the ones that were 60's-sound purists, and the bands that mixed 70's hard rock influences with their 60's punk were certainly despised by the bands that didn't. Having authenticity issues within a culture that no one could accuse ultimately of being particularly authentic seems to be yet another example of a means with which the white middle class titillate themselves.

It must be more trickle-down post-modernity that assemblage in some instances supersedes the original artifact in desirability, but what are you gonna do? If you are all young and all excited, hot and bothered and all that, and when you're done with the porno sites, you can choose to go tooling for garage punk on any of many download/stream sites. You find yourself staring at an event horizon of band names and song titles that provide exactly zilch and bupkis as far as context for the crazy rock & roll that you can (sorta) enjoy on them rin-tin-can speakers on your laptop. How do you navigate? Who can tell you? Blogs provide consumer guidance certainly and no doubt, but François Boucher's ghost pops up jack-in-the-box style and yells that his axiom on nature, "Too green and poorly illuminated"** can be utilized to describe most garage/punk blogs. Fanzines are great but as old ones are hard to find, new ones seem to put more emphasis on collage-art that incorporates Harmony Korine's butt cheeks and less on necessary consumer guidance of primitive musics, and the ones that should be providing that consumer guidance are awfully busy printing

---

** I know I've used this joke before but it is still funny.

extended logorrhea-riffic essays on bands that kind of aren't very good. So: Whatever consumer guidance can be found in the assemblage conducted in days of yore warrants big-price-tag merit. As the 60s punk comps assembled back in the eighties were assembled by fanatix that weren't happy with only indulging their own ears, but utilizing their individual collector frenzy to attempt to contaminate the ears of others, that meritocracy will stay potent evermore, and original copies of *Scum Of The Earth* or *Chosen Few* will often be more expensive than some of the original records compiled on the same.

First comes the *Back From The Grave* series, so:

1. **BFTG #1 (Crypt Records 1983)**
2. **BFTG #5 (Crypt Records 1985)**
3. **BFTG #3 (Crypt Records 1984)**
4. **BFTG #4 (Crypt Records 1984)**
5. **BFTG #8 (Crypt Records 1995)**
6. **BFTG #6 (Crypt Records 1986)**
7. **BFTG #7 (Crypt Records 1988)**
8. **BFTG #2 (Crypt Records 1983)**

And the generous reader can go ahead and jest along the lines of sycophancy and ass-kissing as the shapely buttocks of the Crypt Records executives have continued to drive us wild-wild-wild for the last quarter of a century.

9. **Boulders Volume 1 (Max 1, USA 1979 or 80)**

The Dave Gibson-compiled volume one of the *Boulders* series shouldn't suffer from the same bad reputation as the rest, this one is an all-killer no filler, and came out way back in 1979. And besides: people do beef about the gravelophonic sound quality of the *Boulders* series, but my ears (both attached to my head still) cannot discern anything worse-sounding here than on the *Pebbles* comps.

10.   Everywhere Chainsaw Sound volume 1
       (CSR 001, France 1982)

This early French compilation, sporting a handmade silkscreened
sleeve in an edition of 200 numbered copies, certainly weaves the
DIY-ethic and the importance of the independent record shop into the
grooves of the wax itself: This record is as home-made as any DIY punk
record, and its reverberations of the secret handshakes of record store
back rooms that followed as the logical next step from fanzine articles
and collectors' trading compilation cassettes show the passion of the
chase and the glory of the pay-off in a way most removed from our time
of google-searches and on-line snark. So who cares if there is a bunch
of clunkers on this comp, we are talking 1982 here and Ken and the
Fourth Dimension are blasting out "See If I Care."

11.   Chosen Few Volume 1 (A-Go-Go 1966, USA 1982)
12.   Chosen Few Volume 2 (Tom-Tom 3752, USA 1983)

Chosen Few volume one and two (both compiled by east coast garage
scenester Bruce and released in the early eighties) are tightly assembled
comps, especially if your taste runs to the big riff/big guitar/dare-I-say
pro end of the 60's punk spectrum. Volume one assembles bands that
coulda, woulda and possibly shoulda had albums deals and the level of
notoriety of say the Seeds, the Standells or the Chocolate Watchband.
Notable exceptions are some tracks that showed up on *BFTG* like the
Nomads "Thoughts of a Madman" or "Are You For Real Girl" by the
Mystic Five. Thee Wylde Main-iacs are Erik Lindgren and pals on a
civil war reenactment trek, but remember, this comp came out in '82
and a mere whiff of 16 years had slipped by since 1966 was 1966 and all
music was all 1966. If we want to talk 16 years ago we'd be at "Dookie"
and the death of Kurt Cobain. Ain't it funny how time slips and all,
Erik and his pals sure did a good job faking it and Bruce did an equally
great job defining that which Thee Wylde Main-iacs were faking. Hm.
There's something in there somewhere about my old fave hobby-horse
the Stoic view of time and direction. I'll save that one for my upcoming

blogosphere debut, scheduled for, oh, 16 years from now. Volume two might be even better than volume one, and while still remaining on the bowl-cut tough-guy slant of 60's punk, instead of my preferred slant of psychotic and primitive shit-music a la Modds or Kick Klack or the Keggs, it is an utterly playable comp, perfectly close to dare-I-say Donatello for its finesse and Brancusi for the vision and brute strength of execution.

13   Crude PA volume 1 (Distortions 1001, USA 1990)

14.   Crude PA volume 2 (Distortions 1024, USA 1996)

In the spirit of *BFTG*, this amazing comp focuses on the crude, crazy and inept, all from Pennsylvania. A popular cliché amongst the 80's garage scenesters was the notion that 60's punk/garage musicians were "wild and primitive cavemen," making "wild and primitive noise" and possibly feasting on "primitive cave grub." This reverberated across the globe, possibly helped along the way by copies of "Be A Caveman" by the Avengers (on *Boulders* #1) and posters of Raquel Welch in *One Million Years B.C.* and ended up being a given for how garage people presented their craft. Well: Several tracks on *Crude PA* actually sound like primitive cavemen making wild and primitive noise. And the PA food, from Pat's steaks to a Shoofly Pie at the Dutch Kitchen in Frackville certainly can be interpreted as primitive cave grub. Both volumes of *Crude PA* are blistering masterpieces from out of nowhere, no doubt. Primitive and great.

15   Earpiercing Punk (Trash 0001, USA 1983)

When *EPP* came out, it was a bit of a revelation (after getting past the baffling sleeve wrapped in a pic of a 77-style safety-pin punk babe) that a comp had been released lining up crazed (tough) fifties rockers alongside solid 60's punk tracks. This comp doesn't have the reputation of say, *Scum of the Earth* or *Off the Wall*, but it is pretty damn fantastic, and easy to find as well.

16.   Florida Punk (Eva 12026, France 1983)
17.   Louisiana Punk (Eva 12051, France 1986)
18.   New Mexico Punk (Eva 12047, France 1985)

The Eva Records garage comps that started to flow out of Paris in the early-mid eighties were more often than not put together by Jersey-collector Vic whose ears for sixties punk blaze rivaled those of Tim Warren. The best Eva compilations easily outshine all *Pebbles*, and rival the best early US private press comps. These three all dive-bomb out of your speakers and enter your brain like a perfect espresso. As we will never hear everything, own everything or remember everything, we should all be glad that there are fellows like Vic out there, who shared his gnosis 25-plus years ago.

19.   **Garage Punk Unknowns Volume 4
      (Stone Age no #, USA 1985)**

In some ways, this feels like the lost *BFTG* volume. It is that good. A slew of (still) obscure R&B-punk tracks, this one plays beautifully, the compiler as always avoiding what members of my family refer to as "the hippie quotient," i.e. the presence of incensey/peppermintey clownage intermingling with the hunk of punk on garage comps of an early/mid 80's vintage.

20.   **Off The Wall Volume 1 (Wreckord Wrack 1025, 1982)**
21.   **Off The Wall Volume 2 (Wreckord Wrack 1301, 1983)**

The two volumes of *OTW* have certain whispered somethings to say about the art of assembly, of sequencing, of compiling and its core mystical and alchemical nature. Some comps *work*, and some don't. Some playlists do/don't, mixed tapes for pals, mixed tapes for babes, some work and some don't, and it seems very difficult to discern what components direct the work in one direction or another. As this whiff is being written, I've been spilling a constant stream of garage comps on the turntable, and in a manner waiting for myself to react: not only for a particularly crazy record to entice one to start dancing the frug, but for those sanctified moments where every consecutive record in sequence adds exponential critical mass to the previous until the comp becomes a thing unto itself. *OTW* 1 & 2 deliver in spades. The liner notes of *OTW* 1 consist of as clear and concise statement of definition and intent that we'll ever get about 60's punk and how it came to be: and as it was written in 1981, fifteen years after 1966, I can but gasp that 15 years ago today was 1995 and what odious jams ruled airwaves mainstream and underground that given year. Oh well. What was once directly lived has receded into a representation.

22.   **Open Up Yer Door Volume 1 (Frog Death 101, USA 1984)**

23.   **Open Up Yer Door Volume 2 (Frog Death 102, USA 1987)**

Both superb, compiled with that rare finesse that showcases not only DJ skills, but also access to a serious collection. In the days of record collecting before the internet, you knew what you knew and you had what you had. Some dealers provided cassettes, some collectors as well, some most certainly didn't, and that most exalted gate-keeper/occult-knowledge tomfoolery as always resulted in less enthusiasm being spread and less people having less fun. The gent who compiled these two, and who I used to run into at NYC record shops in the late eighties, always came across as one of those men whose fascination for musical marginalia was infused with such much meaning that all other art-forms and means of human expression faded in comparison. I remember his mega-enthused logorrhea devoted to a meritocracy of primitive teenage two-chord bashing and how I *could simply not wait* to hear the sounds described. *OUYD* vol. 1 & 2 are standing legacies to this gentleman's ability to enthuse, inspire and share.

143

24.   Scum of the Earth Volume 1 (Killdozer 1001, USA 1984)
25.   Scum of the Earth Volume 2 (Killdozer 002, USA 1984)

Oddly enough, *SOTE* vol 1&2 don't really register as garage comps, nor as consumer guides or party soundtracks or, don't know really, they are things unto themselves, works of abject originality, like the Cramps, or a Kurt Schwitters collage. Both volumes positively shimmer with punk rock gnosis: that rare insight that it is all the same anyway and that the transient nature of the everyday means that the blasts spilled on the gramophone are something between us and said blasts, hence it don't really matter what the band wears, what decade they are from, their race or their socio-economical strata.*** Both volumes are loosely divided into a punk-side and a general pre-(60's)-punk weirdness side that are put together with such an insight into the craft of compiling that the natural flow of the comps is so goddamn 24-karat that I think I have the sequence memorized through repeated play over the years.

26.   What a Way to Die (Satan 1313, USA 1983)

WAWTD landed in Swedish record shops in the fall of 1984, after the first couple of volumes of *BFTG*, and right before the *GPU* series. Needless to say, me and my snotty little pals hadn't heard of any of the records on the comp, and were yet again blown away by this constant stream of what could only be described as sacred sounds from the USA (where, we had heard, hamburgers sizzled night and day, a concept most dear to us, as in Sweden the burger joints closed at 4:30 in the afternoon and served up the burgers steamed with a mixture of lingonberry jam and lutefisk on top). I remember wondering if this array of cultural wealth would ever end, and how come most rock (and punk) I'd heard from the sixties to date didn't even come close to the marvelous intensity of the jams on comps like this one. Well: we know now that the early collectors of 60's punk (Todd A. and Vince B. compiled this one) truly were able explorers and through instinct reached many of the most picturesque areas of the landscape, like Lewis and Clark or so.

*** No: scratch that. It does matter what they wear and the quality of the experience will reduce in potency if "keeping-it-real"-sideburns are maintained by the musicians.

27.   Pebbles Volume 9 (BFD Records, USA 1980(?))
28.   Pebbles Volume 1 (BFD Records, USA 197(?), reissued 1979)
29.   Pebbles Volume 7 (BFD Records 5024, USA 1980)
30.   Pebbles Volume 8 (BFD Records 5025, USA 1980)

The release date for *Pebbles* volume one varies a great deal. The Midnight book states 1975. Some claim 1977, Wikipedia states 1978, and not that I don't trust them, but hey, they've sold me swampland more than once. Jon Savage says that Greg Shaw sent him a white label in 1978 so somewhere in that where, a compilation called *Pebbles* came out. *Pebbles* volume one first came out as a white label with a red insert sleeve and was reissued with an album jacket featuring the image of the pinhead that we've all learned to love a few months later. Either way and any way: the re-release of *Pebbles* volume one in 1979, and the consecutive 1980 release of the next ten or so volumes, was timed perfectly with the boost in interest in all-things-sixties that was a snacky side-dish to the powerpop main. The punk-era ears had gotten people used to raunch, and the avalanches of indie 45s had advanced the momentum of obscurity thrill-seeking. The musical language of sixties punk had also nowhere near jelled by 1979. To most, the sixties was pop and choruses and ringing Rickenbackers, and therefore there wasn't a clear idea of otherness, distinguishing the cutesy stuff from the gruntiest and most primitive. This is certainly reflected in the *Pebbles* track listings, as is Greg Shaw's personal taste, with its baffling Geoffrey Weissian adoration of melody. It doesn't feel particularly important or meaningful to point out that the Golem has clay feet. The *Pebbles* series is ultimately fantastic. Important, meaningful, all that. One of my greatest senses of musical wonders experienced as of yet was the turntable spillage of *Pebbles* volume 9, hearing "Project Blue" by the Banshees and "At the Rivers Edge" by New Colony Six for the first time, but this needs to be said: It is odd how poor the musical quality control on *Pebbles* is, especially as one contrasts with the diligent and superb liner notes.****

**** The two part notes on volume 7 and 8 of Pebbles, "The Boy Looked At Roky," is a jaw-dropping, knee-slapping, scotch-spilling slice of equilibrist comical genius where Greg Shaw takes the mega-mickey out of the Burchill/Parsons mega-pretentious speedfreak rant tract on punk The Boy Looked At Johnny.

As the series progressed, the song selections started to include stuff that even the most ardent 60's-fetishist would have a hard time shoehorning down his gullet, and furthermore that an extremely gravel-o-phonic and hap-hazard treatment of the actual sounds compiled, cutting corners in mastering and using versions taken from cassettes instead of masters or original vinyl (performances that were pretty damn low-fidelity in the first place, and quite often pressed up on the vinyl grade that contains a significant percentage of apple-cores and Chinese newspapers). As you may know, some tracks are pitched (most notably the Squires), and the baffling inclusion of "Action Woman" by The Litter with a big ol' skip in the middle is as blatant an illumination as one can possibly hope for whence an old-timer like myself is cornered to explain the nature of obscurity and the difficulty of location when it came to rare vinyl prior to interwebs and brick and mortar shop shutdowns. I can only explain the sliding quality scale of the series and the somewhat sloppy execution of some of the comps as the victim of enthusiasm versus obsession. I think Greg Shaw's intent, vision and diligence was superb: where the problem lies, is when the scholar thinks that it is within his grasp to comprehend and define a complete and comprehensive chain of events and gathering of materials.

The swell record store Finyl Vinyl had a sign on the wall that bore the legend:

You will...
Never know everything
Never hear everything
Never own everything
Never remember everything

But leaving you, handsome reader, with that sentiment is much too dark. Instead, here's a list of paint-peeling, barn-storming, speaker-annihilating cuts from above comps that I hope will function as a plausible consumer guidance exercise in lieu of statements about rarity, rawness and wildness. All these jams can easily be found on the web.

Send the compilers of *Pebbles, Back From The Grave, Nuggets, Off The Wall*, etc. a warm and cozy thought as you visit or revisit some of the most splendid sounds made on our earth beside (natch) those of moaning women and laughing babies.

The Untamed – "Someday Baby" (*Off The Wall* vol. 1)
Electras – "Action Woman" (*Open Up Yer Door* vol. 1)
Keggs – "To Find Out" (*BFTG* 5)
New Colony Six – "At The Rivers Edge" (*Pebbles* 9)
Avengers – "Be A Caveman" (*Boulders* 1)
The Bitters End – "Find Somebody To Love Me" (*Crude PA* 1)
Keith Kessler – "Don't Crowd Me" (*Ear Piercing Punk*)
Alarm Clocks – "No Reason To Complain" (*BFTG* 1)
Chancellors – "On Tour" (*BFTG* 8)
Belles – "Melvin" (*GPU* 4)

2010

17

Notes on an Exhibit I Found Rather Crass

I went and saw an exhibit in New York on the visual legacy of a legendary punk band. I thought that it was put together with a lot of enthusiasm, and it was fascinating to see this highly political work within the walls of a fairly prestigious and pretentious gallery.

I purchased the catalogue, and what I found in it troubled me ever so slightly. I think the curator was interested in contextualizing himself with the work of the band as a means of adding that fluid concept of credibility to his work as a visual artist. The collection on display had recently been purchased by the curator from one of the premier antiquarian booksellers in London, and brought to the USA for exhibit.

With this in mind, I also reflected on a recent exhibit of counter-culture publications of yore. Alongside these artifacts of bohemian life in the fifties through the seventies were placed and sold the recent publications of the curator (not the same guy). Magical thinking, the predominant millennial misery of life in the age of ephemeral knowledge, means that if you place your work in the vicinity of greatness, said greatness will rub off on your work, and your work will be great too. If the devil on your left shoulder says that that is abject bullshit, then the angel on your right shoulder can whisper that even if your underground poetry magazines are the Chef Boy-Ar-Dee version of Ferlinghetti, posterity still won't be able to tell the difference if you reference City Lights and the man himself every chance you can, as your work will then be catalogued and cross-referenced with the work of the great that you wish to slide up alongside. This life-lie can be enough to sustain you and your work throughout your lifetime. Ponder the Warhol cronies; there will always be some exhibit or art festival overseas or in Canada where a personal appearance that includes a moderate honorarium can go down, and there will always be a TV show or a coffee table book or a university symposium where your work can be contextualized with his. Many years ago, I went to the funeral of an entertainment business figure of some renown. This was in the Los Feliz section of Los Angeles. There was a musical performance. A blond thirty-something woman had put together a "celebratory" program of soul- and gospel-infused music to accompany the event. It was deeply uncomfortable. She was rocking out like crazy, chewing the scenery, mustering up all the soul and gospel she could conjure up from the very essence of her being. I remember thinking as I recoiled in horror, that this must be what it felt like watching a blackface minstrel show. It struck me mid-way through that the real agenda was that she was auditioning. She was in a room full of music and film executives, and she had them as her guaranteed audience for the two hours or so of the funeral. She thanked the audience. She thanked the dearly departed. She introduced her band.

A few months ago, at the funeral of an important counter-culture figure, a couple of much less important counter-culture figures were handing out a limited edition "celebratory" signed and numbered CD of their own making. The hubris of contextualizing oneself with past greats is a particularly *o tempora o mores* of our day. As some kind of documentation of the event is sure to mention the signed limited numbered CD that was only available as a homage giveaway, the given victorious mediocrities have succeeded with what they set out to do: the contextualization with the greats based on the entitlement of the mediocre mind in question. Why do they do this? Do they think God and God's pals are going to hold up score-cards, figure-skating-style, as they arrive in heaven and will take their rightful place in the wing of coolness and credibility at the (no doubt) five star heavenly resort? That God and his pals will provide them with all-access laminates so the backstage area in Heaven can be effortlessly accessed? As usual I blame the goddamn internet. The ego-boost of immediate contextualization of your work with the greats of yore is all that is needed. It is no longer of merit to be influenced by legends, what has happened instead is that the performer is working within the contextual narrative of greatness that includes these giants of long-ago, but also him or her. And God and his pals won't be able to notice the difference. The media din is too loud.

A couple of English rock magazines throw yearly award-shows. The awards are straight out of the mind of C. Montgomery Burns, all outstanding awards of achievement in the field of excellence. Some they dole out to legends of the sixties and seventies that happen to still be above ground. These awards are usually handed out by contemporary artists, specifically the ones that have made the loudest tut-tut-noises in the general direction of coolness and credibility in interviews in the magazines that give out the awards. Contextualizing themselves with the celebrated legendary dinosaurs, hoping that as time passes they will also be celebrated as legendary dinosaurs.

The generational depletion of merit in mass culture is doubtlessly caused by how the same culture is not only consumed, but also how it is presented for consumption. Rock and pop are ruled by the baby duck syndrome: If you drag a banana tied to a piece of string in front of a baby duck, the baby duck will think it is his mother. And as we consume most of our music as names in a column, devoid of context, meaning and its historical place, the go-getting interns can kick-start their career by repeatedly declaring their coolness and credibility, and their linearity with the greats, as media and machinery still care, even if the consumers don't really.

2011

18

Velvet Underground Artifacts and Other People's Nostalgia

Artwork born out of necessity, where the artist or producer was not particularly concerned with notoriety or posterity, and a simple vibrant message was projected onto the viewer with all the subtlety of a donut billboard, has provided us with the some of our strongest visual visceral thrills, especially if a few decades have passed since they were executed. These Velvet Underground posters weren't designed by Andy Warhol. Nor were they "approved" by the band or their management or label as congenial to the image branding of the group. They were slapped together to act as advertising for gigs at a time where the poster or flyer in many instances was the *only* channel of communication betwixt a band/venue and the fans/audience. This work is anonymous, and this urgent, necessary and ephemeral anonymity contains some of the most potent narrative strands of the 20th century. It reverberates throughout the decades since, kissing/slapping almost all cultural expressions, be they hi-, lo- or uni-brow that surround us here in the very start of the 21st. Friedrich Schlegel's tasty slice of rhetorical irony dive-bombs here as he pointed out a couple of centuries ago how critical writing is revealing its own artifice by exposing the hand of the creator intruding the text.

The nostalgia that we infuse the artifact with confronts the scratches, dents, fades and imperfections of these legendarily rare posters, and brings about an inner wabi-sabi, where our experience of the eternal now (à la baby-boomer sixties worship) in tangent with the eternal then (where style reigns over substance) in a worst-case scenario gives us a sneaky suspicion that we now live after the end of the world, and all things cool have already happened to other people. In a better-case viewpoint, now that we have 100 years of accumulated pop culture at our fingertips, we shall always feel psyched up and motivated cuz there's always so much cool stuff around to inspire us.

The apparent downside of the baby-boomer stranglehold on popular culture has a substantial upside, which is communication over generations. When a 2009 16-year old responds viscerally to the style, substance and wabi-sabi of these Velvet Underground posters, thereby gaining a commonality of taste with previous generations, whether that commonality remains on the surface à la "cool poster" or sinks deep à la "the Velvet Underground are the best band I've ever heard!," then new alliances are forged, and one can supersede the us-versus-them basics of generational mutuality and replace them with something that to this mind looks an awful lot like communication.

In October of 2009, noted art book publisher Rizzoli issued an artists monograph devoted to the Velvet Underground. This tome, which I edited, I think is a hint of more to come. The popular arts of the latter half of the 20th century are more and more being contextualized alongside the fine art movements of the 20th century, and it ain't always so easy to tell the difference between fine and popular, hi-brow, lo-brow or uni-brow. This is the first time that an artist's monograph has been issued for a 20th century rock band. It is no surprise that the subject for the very first one is the Velvet Underground, as the entire web-work plot I've spun in this yarn of an article goes out the window when you see the face of a young person light up when they hear the Velvet Underground for the first time as a reminder that our strongest art experiences are visceral.

2009

19

Malcolm McLaren has Left the 20th Century

Malcolm McLaren died on April 10th of 2010 at the age of 64.

He left us behind, still correlating and contextualizing the map ("The Map is On the Territory") and the manual ("Believe in the Ruins"[9]) of his visionary ultra-potency. The Situationists have been described as the phantom avant-garde. They didn't leave many physical materials behind, unlike say the Surrealists or the Expressionists or the mail-art folks or the Fluxus crew who all made *things*. Things that were *for sale* or *given away*: that exchanged hands, that remained behind after movements dissolved or disappeared or people died. With the Situationists, the potency of the ideas in the texts of Raoul Vaneigem or Guy Debord or Constant Nieuwenheus (and all their pals-enemies-frenemies) are increasing in strength and actuality for every month that passes by.

Most universities worth their weight in vegan cheeseburgers will teach a class or two that touch upon Situationist thought, and the editorial staff of publishing houses like this one will sigh "ah, yes" and reach for the daily lunch pint upon their mention. And all tweaked kidding aside, there is little doubt that we permanently reside in a society of the spectacle and that the New Babylon[10] resides in our collective homes spreading a blue-ish glow, providing news, communication with loved ones, and a side of compulsive shopping and/or masturbation. Constant Nieuwenheus probably saw that one coming.

"Then what about punk, then?" murmurs the everyman punk from his squat (or condo) in Stoke-Newington. "*Very complex…*" I mumble and reach for Guy Debord's favorite brand of calvados. The psycho-geography of Malcolm McLaren's life and work can't be easily pinned down, as his instrumental super-power in the mass distribution of potent and subversive strands of feel-thought is a *derivé*—a drift—and as such, as aimless as the Roman stoics found our directionless journey from cradle to grave. Upon McLaren's consecutive creations of myriads of situations, situations that echo and reverberate and clang all over the

---

9 "Believe in the Ruins" was one of the six banners used to promote *The Great Rock & Roll Swindle*.
10 "New Babylon": Constant Nieuwenheus' theories of the Situationist city.

roadmaps covering the territories of our everyday lives, we collectively add to their psycho-geography.

The situations we create in their continuation that are revolutionary or subversive or inspired or self-starter do not belong to the past, to the 20th century, or to McLaren as the *détournement*[11] continues as we *détourne* that which in turn was *détourned* by a previous generation. And as every avant-garde grows old and dies, without necessarily being able to recognize its successor, as Asger Jorn said, one must think that Malcolm had no idea of how much change he set in motion, or how little reward he would get from it. Or maybe he was rewarded, in fact "Paid in Full" à la the Eric B and Rakim short-story. Paid in full in the sense that he seemingly never worked, maintaining the Homo Ludens existence we can all only hope for.

The residual objects left behind by this one-man phantom avant-garde are ephemeral, but they do exist. What is chosen to be presented is meant to illustrate our privilege of having been shown and told things at random by this anarchic and chaotic artist.

This artist who in his life and work whispered secret truths about the equally anarchic and chaotic half-century that we are so desperately incapable of leaving.

We can't get up and bail until we've learned to interpret the signs and sigils left behind by those brave, those few, those chosen who figured out how to depart it. There is no way that we can possibly understand how radical the act of designing these t-shirts, the act of buying them or the act of wearing them was in London 1975/1976. Our event-horizon is absolute, our view of past life is static, and imagery is only screen-flicker and beauty stored by Flickr on your computer screen. This imagery, equal in its sublime and subversive eye-ball-pleasing purity, can no

longer be experienced first-hand by me or you or your mom as they

---

11 *Détournement* is the reuse of preexisting artistic elements in a new ensemble.

have been deconstructed via the attrition of memory, the dusk of punk rock nostalgia, and the thick veneer of art/fashion crowd decadent self-titillation. A *détournement* that perhaps is automatic once all that was once directly lived has receded into a representation.

McLaren's artworks as a young Situationist-infected student in Croydon College and St. Martin School of the Arts certainly yearn and hint at the shape of punk to come, and the sublime deconstruct of the music product marketing *détournement* of the Sex Pistols and Bow Wow Wow, and the World Famous Supreme Team (as well as the man himself), is in my mind no less inspiring than Asger Jorn and Guy Debord's *Fin de Copenhague* or Marcel Duchamp's ready-mades. Late at night, at bed time, after you've listened to Marie Osmond's reading of Hugo Ball's "Karawane"[12] on a sequenced playlist with Bow Wow Wow's "C-30 C-60 C-90 Go" followed by Chuck Berry's "Let It Rock,"[13] you might agree with me that Malcolm McLaren was a direct successor of Duchamp, and that Punk follows Dada and Situationism. What was once directly lived might unfortunately now mostly have receded into representations, but if we choose to *détourne* our past we are no longer forced to repeat it. Please pay homage to Malcolm McLaren and inform yourself of his random stream of situations and possibilities, it would sure be nice to commence this 21st century that we've heard so much about.

2010

---

12 http://www.youtube.com/watch?v=JVpjIJ8a9cA
13 McLaren named his first clothing shop after his favorite record.

20

Baron Corvo – The Greatest Asshole that Ever Lived

Frederick Rolfe AKA Baron Corvo, 1860 - 1913 has been called:

A wasted genius
An eccentric and curious artist
A man with only the very vaguest sense of realities
An unhappy Catholic vagabond
A writer of challenging gifts and powers

When I try to get friends and acquaintances sucked into the void of Corvo-fandom, or more like it, fanaticism, I have to explain the fascination of the asshole. An asshole is not someone who physically harms people, or kills people; those folks are just scum. Like Aleister Crowley. No fun to collect first editions, no fun to dissect his books over brandy next to the fireplace, no fun to repeat anecdotes from his notorious life. Crowley is scum.

Frederick Rolfe, AKA Baron Corvo, on the other hand, might be the biggest asshole that ever lived, a true asshole, in the sense of Bataille's *Solar Annulus*, where the inmost light shines forth from the bung so brightly we must call it the sun. Where, like the *Merde Celebre* end results from conceptual art legend Wim Delvoye's *Cloaca* machine warrant a price tag of a couple of thousand pounds, and that for a piece of machine-made shit sealed in clear plastic. Where the novels, letters, short stories and essays written by a man who must have been such a deeply narcissistic, smug, megalomaniacal piece of work that he alienated every friend he ever had does not in the slightest take away from the ecstatic bliss of his overheated writing. Rather the opposite, in fact.

Passing judgment on the life of another does reduce that person to a cartoon. Maybe we cannot pass judgment on anyone but ourselves. The casting of stones. With Corvo, the life, letters and vitriol of the man could have stepped out of Dickens, if Dickens had been Lautréamont. It is difficult to think of Frederick Rolfe AKA Baron Corvo as anything but a character who stepped out of a picaresque novel. We are coming up on 92 years since his death, penniless and obscure in a Venice apartment at the age of 53. How he arrived there, and how he spent the time since his first entrance into the world through the portals he despised, reads like, well, a Corvo novel. And it should: Baron Corvo's books are about Baron Corvo like Joni Mitchell songs are about Joni Mitchell and Lester Bangs record reviews are about Lester Bangs. Where the narcissism of Mitchell or Bangs either tires you or leaves you amused, Corvo's brand are like riding the harshest roller coaster at New Jersey's Six Flags while enjoying grade A mescaline. That good. He is to date the unsurpassed master of the ritualized insult, where his maledicta is like the roar of Szechuan peppercorns: at first you don't notice the heat.

But wait a little bit. The blaze rips you like a vintage Greg Ginn guitar solo, especially when he is thrashing one of his real life enemies in fictionalized form. But it ain't all heat: Corvo is also an ecstatic poet, where the descriptions, flavors and nuances of his characters, manners and locations regularly brush against perfection. They can be as pastoral and subtle as Vaughn Williams or raging pure expression impossible to forget. Susan Sontag and Graham Greene, a couple of certified clever bastards, loved Corvo's prose, and both considered his novel *The Desire and Pursuit of the Whole* to be the greatest novel written about the city of Venice. Greene wrote that the book had "the quality of a medieval mystery play, but with this difference, that the play is written from the devil's side." Colin Wilson, who wasn't a Corvo fan, quipped: "Rolfe is a man about whom I could argue at great length with his admirers. Perhaps this in itself is a back-handed testimony in favour of his life and works."

Corvo studied to be a priest, but the Catholic Church threw him out, because he was too much of a weirdo, pedophile and non-reality-based paranoiac. Too much of a piece of work for the Catholic Church, and I don't have to finish that sentence. He wrote short stories for *The Yellow Book*, he painted religious banners with boy-saint motifs. He had a poem included in the legendary Uranian rarity *Love in Earnest* which he forced the publisher to manually remove post-publication because of a quarrel with the editor. He wrote a whirling dervish of a confusing factoid-marinated mess of a book about the Borgias, only to demand that the publishing house remove his name from the project when they dared to edit him. He borrowed money from everybody and repaid no one.

He posed and swaggered as a nobleman-in-dire-straits—that most delicious cliché—when his humble lower middle class beginnings failed to fulfill his ache for the picturesque. He photographed teenage boys in the nude. He made enemies left and right and cherished them. He invented hundreds of words. He swore himself to celibacy for 20 years, and when they were up lead a life of debauchery in Venice (which he wrote about in the legendary and infamous triple-X *Venice Letters*) that would have Terry Richardson hang up his schlong. He wrote myriads of articles for myriads of magazines. He became a published author in 1901 with a reprint of the stories that had appeared in *The Yellow Book* as *Stories Toto Told Me*, which was followed by *In His Own Image*, a book so splendidly fucked, multi-layered and meta that a hundred JT Leroy's on a hundred kinds of narcotics on a hundred typewriters for a hundred years shouldn't bother.

In 1904, Corvo's *Hadrian the Seventh* was published, and the first of Corvo's wish-fulfillment books had seen the day of light. The plot of this strange and powerful novel, with its insights and illuminations of obscure aspects of the Vatican, consists in a nutshell of Corvo becoming Pope. The ensuing hi-jinx are oddly modern, and creepily timely, not to mention obsessive in a manner that predates Kerouac by half a century and also surpasses him in dare-I-say modernist prose. On July 14th of 2004 a bunch of book-dealing swells hosted by Ed Maggs celebrated the centenary of its publication with a luncheon at the Academy in Soho. Graham Greene called the book a work of genius.

D.H. Lawrence stated: "If it is the book of a demon as Corvo's contemporaries said, it is the book of a man demon, not a mere poseur. And if some of it is caviar, at least it came out of the belly of a live fish." *Hadrian the Seventh* has been in print for more or less a century. Read the damn thing, please.

In 1905 Fr. Robert Hugh Benson, one of the three literary Benson brothers and the son of the Archbishop of Great Britain, befriended Corvo. The predestined pattern of the Corvine friendship commenced: raging enthusiasm, discussions of collaborations, petty quarrels that grew into raging animosity. Baron Corvo arrived to Venice in August of 1908 on holiday with a friend. He was never to leave. Here, he celebrated his greatest feats of decadent debauchery, of sordid material extravagance, and wrote *The Desire and Pursuit of the Whole*; arguably the most Corvine of his books. He also starved, froze, went homeless, appeared at death's door not once but several times, borrowed money from everybody, alienated his friends, his enemies, his landlord, and the green grocer, all documented in its shabby glory in that most delirious book about the most delirious city. Set against the backdrop of Corvo's creepiest and most idealized wish fulfillment: The adoring and eternal love of a strapping young gondolier, half-bakedly presented in the book as an adolescent girl. The maledicta aimed steadily against his true-life enemies is as fireworks as it gets, but the descriptions of the magic city are unfuckwithable:

"The lengthy line of lights along Spinalonga fluttered like little pale daffodils in a night-mist coloured like the bloom on the fruit of the vine."

Corvo died in October of 1913 and was close to forgotten as an author by the end of the Great War. A.J.A. Symons, a great eccentric in his own right, was a brilliant dilettante who had started the First Edition Club and the Food and Wine Society, and who had developed a great expertise in Victorian literature. Corvo became his obsession, his quest, and in 1934 Symons's classic book *The Quest For Corvo* was published and met with great enthusiasm. The book, which is in print to this day through Penguin, can be called the birth of the modern biography and is a masterpiece of layered realities and an exploration of the dynamic between author and subject which certainly merits comparison to Boswell and Johnson. More and more Corvine reprints followed; some were extremely limited fine print editions, and some were mostly circulating in gay bookish circles. Two more biographies followed as well as extensive commentaries and finagling of ultra-minutiae. The clichéd outcry of the genius, misunderstood and unappreciated during his lifetime, did in Corvo's case come true: every letter, receipt, scribble and note has become a valued artifact, argued over by scholars and enthusiasts alike.

Some Corvo Greatest Hits:

On R.H. Benson:
He did not exactly aspire to actual creation; but he certainly nourished the notion that several serious mistakes had resulted from his absence during the events described in the first chapter of Genesis.

From a letter to Fr. Beauclerk:
As for the psychic bitterness which you fancy you have detected in me, if my garden produces wormwood, it is because an enemy has sowed the seeds among my lavender.

From a letter to publisher Grant Richards:
By all, to whom I name your name, you are despised or hated; but I doubt whether you ever have made a more ruthless or persequent enemy than -- Your obedient Servant Frederick William Rolfe

From a letter to C.H.C. Pirie-Gordon:
I disdain your dirty pusillanimous poltroonery.

From a letter to C.H.C. Pirie-Gordon:
I am now simply engaged in dying as slowly and as publicly and as annoyingly to all you professing and non-practicing friends of mine.

From a letter to an unknown recipient:
What do you mean by letting a Quaker go rooting and snouting in my lovely Catholic garden?

21

Post-Good Artist Makes
A Good Sculpture

Or Is It A Book?

I've been enjoying Richard Prince's latest sculpture a lot: It is made of paper, glue and ink. It looks like a book, it also reads like a book, a real good book, "the Catcher in the Rye" by JD Salinger. In fact, it looks a lot like a copy of the second edition of "the Catcher in the Rye", except it has Richard Prince's name on it instead of Salinger, and it lists other books by Richard Prince on the inside. The 1951 first edition of "the Catcher in the Rye" has a photograph of JD Salinger on the back of the dustcover, and this pissed Salinger off in a mighty way, as he didn't like phoniness, so it was replaced by a nothing on subsequent editions. The 2011 Richard Prince first edition has replaced the kit and caboodle with a big phony nothing that states that the book (sculpture!) is a work of art, even if it looks pretty much like the real thing, and that brings me to the conclusion that this is the book of the year as "the Catcher in the Rye" sells hundreds of thousands of copies each year and Richard Prince's artworks sell for hundreds of thousands of dollars.

Every age gets the Duchamp it deserves, and we have one that just made us his own readymade. It is a book. It is a sculpture. Book! Sculpture! Readymade! Fraud! Art! Book! Sculpture!

The rapture has come to pass, and we are the ones left behind. All that was good in the world has left and gone to heaven, so we are now surrounded by artwork, music, films, books and sculptures that are Post-Good. Post-Good artists make Post-Good art, Post-Good authors write Post-Good books, and Post-Good magazines publish Post-Good writers etc. Richard Prince is Post-Good, as notions of 'good' and 'bad' have exactly nothing to do with his work. Any of his work.

His early work is embryonically Post-Good (it still incorporates elements of good), his most well-known recent appropriation artworks found hanging on the walls of major museums are milestones of Post-Good, since his work has matured and no longer shows any traces of good. The influx of bad that could be found in some of his early work can also that no longer be clearly discerned, which the critics and dealers and museum curators and wealthy art patrons all seem to have noted. The reader could find it half-interesting if I mention that Richard Prince's recent book of Post-Good essays is currently setting the pace for other artists, writers and critics who work in the Post-Good field.

I am hoping that Richard Prince's sculpture (that looks like a book) was sculpted (printed) to piss off Deborah Batts, a judge who recently ruled that Richard Prince was a biter for biting some portrait photographs of Rastafarians by a marginal photographer, and then using them as the basis for some of his collages that his gallerist Larry Gagousian sold for some of those hundreds of thousands of dollars a couple of years ago.

Deborah Batts is a Post-Good judge, and her ruling in the case of Richard Prince verses the photographer of Rastafarians show Post-Intelligent insight into how freedom of expression works in fine art of the Post-Good era. Deborah Batts made it clear during the actual court proceedings that she didn't "like" Richard Prince's "art" which truly is a Post-Intelligent yardstick for the relationship between court, copyright and artist. The very same judge ruled against an unauthorized sequel to "the Catcher in the Rye" a couple of years ago, and that ruling in turn shows how able Deborah Batts also is thinking Post-Intelligently on matters of freedom of speech. In 2009, Deborah Batts slapped some poor Swedish author silly who had written a book commenting on Salinger and his relationship to "the Catcher in the Rye" through a narrative that imagined an aged Holden Caulfield as lonely and sad and Salinger as trapped by his own legend. According to Deborah Batts, the Swedish author was a phony telling this kind of story was infringing on the right of the author, and was an attempt to make hundreds of thousands on the JD Salinger legacy. For chrissake.

In a day and age where appropriating images, referencing famous works and biting big chunks from those days prior to the rapture when things could still be good instead of Post-Good, our freedoms need to be fought for more than ever. God bless Richard Prince, the best Post-Good artist working today.

2011

Afterword

"In Dreams Begin Irresponsibilities"
Jack Womack

The title of this afterword is a direct quote from the first essay in this *sui generis* -- meaning, in this context: *most excellent* -- collection, "Michael Jackson is Dead, alas."

Since the days when the Romans admired their finely sculpted Greek statues as they beat their Athenian helots senseless, everyone has imagined that the era in which they live cannot help but be lacking, compared to the great era they managed to just miss. (Burt Lancaster in *Atlantic City*: "You should have seen the ocean back then. It was something.") San Francisco will never be the city it was before the earthquake, Europe no more the peace-loving farrago of kingdoms it was prior to the summer of 1914, and that perfect country called the USA lost its innocence for the seventeenth time by noon, September 11, 2001.

In the thirties Depression-battered folk dreamed of gilded dining rooms, wasp-waisted yet large bustled soubrettes, braces of squabs and limitless bowls of terrapin and green turtle soup, but in those places they would never sup. In the early sixties gray-flannelled Madison Avenue, fearful that their bosses would find their gray ties a tenth of an inch too wide could imagine the day when they'd have known the passwords for every speakeasy, could enjoy bad whiskey served in broken cups, would admire their brown and white spectators and have at their sides girls with Louise Brooks hair wearing dresses indistinguishable from pink teddies; but neither fancy shoes nor lacy step-ins would they ever slip off. Even those who actually used the bathroom at CBGBs have managed, since, to convince themselves that it was a place fondly to be missed; and those who never saw it can only imagine its splendor.

Hear me: the only Golden Age you'll ever know is the one you're living in. A crueler aspect of life is that you tend to realize this only in memory, when you begin to think that everything you knew twenty or thirty years before was shinier, easier, cheaper, more satisfying. But any given Golden Age is, in essence, a 45 cut by some group of teenagers in Ohio in 1959 clocking in at 1:47: brilliant, fast, repeatable only so long as the record holds up, and in no way duplicatable.

In early 1977, some months before I moved to New York, I prepared myself for what I already knew was an ongoing Golden Age (Ramones! Patti Smith! CBGB's bathroom!), making my own hepcat t-shirt by 1) buying a white t-shirt at Woolworth's and black dye; 2) dying the t-shirt black, which was the only way you could get a black t-shirt, then, outside New York; 3) scrawling across it in legible yet perfectly jagged writing, in white ink that chipped away with the first wearing, the words CULT FIGURE. Once in New York I discovered that Max's was closed, the good bands were already playing elsewhere, the Chelsea's weekly rates were too much for a bookstore employee's salary, and it was commonplace to be walking Fifth Avenue in broad daylight and have a group of youth decide to heave bricks at you for no particular reason. Downtown, you could stroll St. Mark's Place and see plainly that the commodification of Bohemia had already begun – begun sometime around 1919, I suspect.

In these wide-ranging essays Johan recognizes, honors (and occasionally slaps around, deservedly) the worthy folk who often fall between the cracks or go wholly unrecognized during any given Golden Age, only to have their perfect hipness perceived by the perfectly hip only when it no longer matters; or when one such as Michael Jackson begins to out-Elvis Elvis in terms of living the maddest life possible and enters realms not visited since the days of Caligula, had Caligula had access to black credit cards and psychotropic drugs; or when a few withdraw entirely from their society to burn down historic churches, simply because if they didn't do it, who would? In providing these thoughts and these accounts, Johan preserves for a short time a bit longer some of the aspects of the Gone World that few noticed then, or notice now, but are worthy of commemorating: for as go Victorian vitrines displaying arrangements of ferns and stuffed weasels, or a bespoke suit made by Taunitz in the 1930s, or the perfectly shiny jacket that wrapped round a fresh copy of *The Big Sleep* the day it went on sale, so goes Popular Culture. Enjoy it while it's here, because whatever you think will last longest won't.

In the last twenty years, as every inch of what William Gibson has called the World's Attic was retrieved, cleaned off, sorted, given a price estimate, and placed securely on high shelves, simultaneously true originality for a time seemed to fade away; so much of the past had been so forgotten, or ignored, that it seemed essential to either recreate it -- a mug's game if ever there was one -- or try and preserve it in toto: equally impossible, eventually tragic. "Everything is coming back," the late George W.S.Trow's friend told him, in the late seventies, as he relates in his short masterwork *In the Context of No Context*, "and then it's never coming back again."

Johan and I were mutual friends of a Master of Popular Culture— possibly, the Master. One who, idly queried regarding the bass player for the Ventures, would reply: "The studio Ventures or the touring Ventures?" One day our friend died, gone before he hit the floor, having just lugged up five flights yet another bag weighted down with LPs rescued from some curbside on Rivington or Essex, because if he didn't do it, who would? *Enthousiasmos* is too often the A-side of *thanatos*.

In the popular mind science fiction is supposed to be predictive, but even as science fiction writers throw up their hands and say no, no, no— in truth the answer is yes, but in reverse. The bright shiny rockets may have been aimed at Mars and Venus, but landed instead on Hackney and Limehouse. Utopian dreams become dystopian actualities in the blink of an eye. People live not in the harsh environment of the moon, but in the harsh environments of the garbage dumps of Cairo and the favelas of Brazil. It is a safe bet that if a science fiction writer *does* appear to be predicting something, the opposite will surely take place. As the 20th century visions of science fiction at last become the 21st century's reality, it turns out that living in the future is harder and less fun than anyone would have ever dared to predict, it seems to us. After postcyberpunk the deluge, and we find ourselves awash in an ever-rising flood. But surely the 20th Century seemed the same, to those who remembered the 19th.

So we turn to fantasy, to reverie, to nostalgia, to dreams; create alternate realities in which we think we can live; but these are highs one grows used to terribly fast, and soon, dreamland is the only place you find yourself able to live. But there you cannot live.

Herein Johan speaks of another deceased friend of his, an artist I never had the chance to meet, "the art execution of the man child can never compete with the artistic endeavor and primary art experiences of your own child." And this is so. Not even the most splendid Caravaggio can ultimately compare with the primal creation: of watching a human being slide into this troublesome existence, but with guidance and love slowly taking shape over the years, prepared as much as possible for the only world he or she will know, while yours will mostly remain to them ever after a mystery. And those who experience this know well that this is the only Golden Age whose passing you are entirely too aware of as it happens, even as its passing is barely perceptible. And when that Golden Age passes as do they all into the Gone World, the children you have watched grow into worthy adulthood will grumble, wishing at times that they had been around when things were *really* fabulous. There will always be a dock, and a green light at the end of it.

But this shouldn't mean the work of the studio Ventures (or, the touring Ventures) should be forgotten -- at least, until it is. And Johan knows that; so let us enjoy the boffins of the London record shows, the escapades of Baron Corvo, the transformation of mimeographed SF fanzines into mimeographed garage band fanzines, and the *Rock en el Chopo* triple LP. They will not be here forever.

Nor, will we.

Contemporary culture has eliminated both the concept of the public and the figure of the intellectual. Former public spaces – both physical and cultural – are now either derelict or colonized by advertising. A cretinous anti-intellectualism presides, cheerled by expensively educated hacks in the pay of multinational corporations who reassure their bored readers that there is no need to rouse themselves from their interpassive stupor. The informal censorship internalized and propagated by the cultural workers of late capitalism generates a banal conformity that the propaganda chiefs of Stalinism could only ever have dreamt of imposing. Zer0 Books knows that another kind of discourse – intellectual without being academic, popular without being populist – is not only possible: it is already flourishing, in the regions beyond the striplit malls of so-called mass media and the neurotically bureaucratic halls of the academy. Zer0 is committed to the idea of publishing as a making public of the intellectual. It is convinced that in the unthinking, blandly consensual culture in which we live, critical and engaged theoretical reflection is more important than ever before.